**Universität Stuttgart**

Architecture-Aware Online Failure Prediction for Software Systems

Von der Fakultät für Informatik, Elektrotechnik und Informationstechnik der Universität Stuttgart zur Erlangung der Würde eines Doktors der Naturwissenschaften (Dr. rer. nat.) genehmigte Abhandlung

Vorgelegt von

Teerat Pitakrat

aus Trang, Thailand

Hauptberichter: Dr.-Ing. André van Hoorn

Mitberichter: Assoc. Prof. Dr. Vittorio Cortellessa

Mitberichter: Prof. Dr. rer. nat. Dr. h. c. Kurt Rothermel

Tag der mündlichen Prüfung: 16.04.2018

Institut für Softwaretechnologie

2018

Herstellung und Verlag:
BoD- Books on Demand, Norderstedt
ISBN: 978-3-7528-7651-2

Abstract

Failures at runtime in complex software systems are inevitable because these systems usually contain a large number of components. Having all components working perfectly at the same time is, if at all possible, very difficult. Hardware components can fail and software components can still have hidden faults waiting to be triggered at runtime and cause the system to fail.

Existing online failure prediction approaches predict failures by observing the errors or the symptoms that indicate looming problems. This observable data is used to create models that can predict whether the system will transition into a failing state. However, these models usually represent the whole system as a monolith without considering their internal components.

This thesis proposes an architecture-aware online failure prediction approach, called HORA. The HORA approach improves online failure prediction by combining the results of failure prediction with the architectural knowledge about the system. The task of failure prediction is split into predicting the failure of each individual component, in contrast to predicting the whole system failure. Suitable prediction techniques can be employed for different types of components. The architectural knowledge is used to deduce the dependencies between components which can reflect how a failure of one component can affect the others. The failure prediction and the component dependencies are combined into one model which employs Bayesian network theory to represent failure propagation. The combined model is continuously updated at runtime and makes predictions for individual components, as well as inferring their effects on other components and the whole system.

The evaluation of component failure prediction is performed on three different experiments. The predictors are applied to predict component failures in a microservice-based application, critical events in Blue Gene/L supercomputer, and computer hard drive failures. The results show that the failures of individual components can be accurately predicted. The evaluation of the whole HORA approach is carried out on a microservice-based application. The results show that the HORA approach, which combines component failure prediction and architectural knowledge, can predict the component failures, their effects on other parts of the system, and the failures of the whole service. The HORA approach outperforms the monolithic approach that does not consider architectural knowledge and can improve the area under the Receiver Operating Characteristic (ROC) curve by 9.9%.

Zusammenfassung

Ausfälle von komplexen Softwaresystemen sind unvermeidbar, weil diese Systeme aus einer Vielzahl von Komponenten bestehen. Es ist schwierig, wenn überhaupt möglich, alle Komponenten gleichzeitig vollkommen funktionierend zu haben. Hardware-Komponenten können ausfallen und Software-Komponenten können noch versteckte Fehler haben, die während der Laufzeit aktiviert werden könnten und zu einem Ausfall des Systems führen.

Existierende Ansätze zur Vorhersage von Laufzeitfehlern sind in der Lage, Ausfälle durch Beobachtung von Fehlern oder Symptomen, die die entstehenden Probleme indizieren, vorherzusagen. Diese erhobenen Daten werden verwendet, um Modelle zu erzeugen, die vorhersagen, ob das System in einen Ausfallzustand übergehen wird. Allerdings repräsentieren diese Modelle das gesamte System als Monolith, ohne die internen Komponenten zu berücksichtigen.

Diese Dissertation stellt einen Ansatz zur Laufzeit-Fehlervorhersage namens HORA vor, der die Architektur explizit berücksichtigt. HORA verbessert die Laufzeit-Fehlervorhersage durch die Kombination von Ergebnissen der Ausfallvorhersage einzelner Komponenten und Informationen über die Systemarchitektur. Die Aufgabe der Ausfallvorhersage ist die Vorhersage der Fehler einzelner Komponenten, nicht jedoch der Ausfall des gesamten Systems. Passende Vorhersageverfahren können für unterschiedliche Typen von Komponenten verwendet werden. Die Architekturinformationen werden verwendet, um die Abhängigkeiten zwischen Komponenten, die bei einem Ausfall Auswirkungen auf andere Komponenten haben, abzuleiten. Die Ausfallvorhersagen und die Komponentabhängigkeiten werden in einem Modell kombiniert, das Bayesian Networks verwendet, um die Fehlerausbreitung zu repräsentieren. Das kombinierte Modell wird während der Laufzeit kontinuierlich aktualisiert und sagt sowohl die Fehler von einzelnen Komponenten als auch die Auswirkungen auf andere Komponenten und Ausfälle des gesamten Systems vorher.

Die Evaluation der Ausfallvorhersage einzelner Komponenten wurde mit drei Systemen durchgeführt, in denen Komponentenausfälle einer Microservice-basierten Anwendung, kritische Ereignisse in dem Blue Gene/L-Supercomputer und Festplattenausfälle vorhergesagt wurden. Die Ergebnisse zeigen, dass die Ausfälle einzelner Komponenten gut vorhergesagt werden können. Die Evaluation des gesamten HORA-Ansatzes wurde mit einer Microservice-basierten Anwendung durchgeführt. Die Ergebnisse zeigen, dass der HORA-Ansatz die Ausfälle einzelner Komponenten, die Auswirkungen auf andere Teile des Systems haben, und die Ausfälle des gesamten Services vorhersagen kann. Der HORA-Ansatz übertrifft den monolithischen Ansatz, der die Informationen über die Systemarchitektur nicht berücksichtigt, und verbessert die Fläche unterhalb der Receiver Operating Characteristic (ROC)-Kurve um 9.9%.

CONTENTS

Publication List

Parts of the material in this thesis have previously appeared in the following publications:

- T. Pitakrat, D. Okanović, A. van Hoorn, and L. Grunske. "Hora: Architecture-aware online failure prediction." In: *Journal of Systems and Software* 137 (2018), pp. 669–685

- T. F. Düllmann, R. Heinrich, A. v. Hoorn, T. Pitakrat, J. Walter, and F. Willnecker. "CASPA: A platform for comparability of architecture-based software performance engineering approaches." In: *International Conference on Software Architecture Workshops (ICSAW)*. 2017, pp. 294–297

- T. Pitakrat, D. Okanovic, A. van Hoorn, and L. Grunske. "An architecture-aware approach to hierarchical online failure prediction." In: *Proceedings of the 12th International ACM SIGSOFT Conference on Quality of Software Architectures (QoSA)*. IEEE. 2016, pp. 60–69

- T. Pitakrat, A. van Hoorn, and L. Grunske. "Increasing dependability of component-based software systems by online failure prediction (short paper)." In: *Proceedings of the 10th European Dependable Computing Conference (EDCC)*. IEEE. 2014, pp. 66–69

- T. Pitakrat, J. Grunert, O. Kabierschke, F. Keller, and A. van Hoorn. "A framework for system event classification and prediction by means of machine learning." In: *Proceedings of the 8th International Conference on Performance Evaluation Methodologies and Tools (VALUETOOLS)*. ICST (Institute for Computer Sciences, Social-Informatics and Telecommunications Engineering). 2014, pp. 173–180

- T. Pitakrat, A. van Hoorn, and L. Grunske. "A comparison of machine learning algorithms for proactive hard disk drive failure detection." In: *Proceedings of the 4th International ACM Sigsoft Symposium on Architecting Critical Systems (ISARCS)*. ACM. 2013, pp. 1–10

- T. Pitakrat. "Hora: online failure prediction framework for component-based software systems based on Kieker and Palladio." In: *Symposium on Software Performance. Joint Kieker/Palladio Days*. 2013, pp. 39–48

Contents

INTRODUCTION

1.1. Problem Statement

Software has become a part of our daily life and plays an important role in many activities. It is embedded in almost everything that we interact with, such as smartphones, wearable devices, computers, automobiles, vending machines, and robots. These devices or machines need to interact and communicate with each other to provide the desired functions. For example, a smart watch can record body movements and count the number of steps of a person. This data can be presented to the user by providing a viewing functionality on the device itself. However, the data can be uploaded to a server to be presented on any device, such as a mobile phone or a computer. Further statistics can be computed by a more powerful device to provide more sophisticated results or combined with data collected from other sources. To achieve the described functionalities, every device and machine needs to operate reliably and correctly.

Avizienis et al. [ALRL04] define a failure as a deviation of a service from the correct service. Although software development processes have been improved in the recent years by quality assurance [Sch08; Tia05], faults can still exist in production software. When these faults are triggered at runtime, they can cause a failure, e.g., performance degradation or service outage that is noticeable by users. The effect of a failure can range from very minimal to catastrophic. For instance, a failure of a music service or internet radio can cause user dissatisfaction while a failure of an online backup service can cause a business to lose revenue. On the other hand, a failure in the control system of a power plant can cause a catastrophic disaster that results in loss of life.

Online failure prediction [SLM10] aims to foresee looming failures at runtime before they manifest themselves. It analyzes the data available at runtime to make a prediction whether a component or a system is going to fail in the very near future. Accurate failure predictions are a prerequisite for preemptive maintenance actions, reducing the effect of problems or even completely preventing them from occurring [BBEM15; CGK+11; CKF+04; LL06]. Existing online failure prediction approaches predict failures either of the whole system or of specific parts of the system. These approaches employ monolithic models which either view each component or the whole system as one entity and predict failure events based on externally observable measurements, e.g., response time [ACG12; CDC10], event logs [PGK+14; SM07], or system metrics [BLM+12; WPN07].

When faced with complex software systems composed of a large number of internal and external components, the existing approaches may not be able to properly analyze all the measurements from components that contribute to the failures. For instance, system failures, which are visible to users, usually originate from complex interactions of erroneous components inside the system. These internal errors, which can be regarded as failures on the component level, can propagate to other parts of the system through the architectural dependencies. This causes a chain of errors up to the system boundary and results in a failure on the system level [ALRL04; CG07; HJS01; JS05; Nyg18]. Thus, without considering the architecture or dependencies between components, these approaches are able to predict only the component failures but not their consequences on other parts of the system.

1.2. Motivating Example

Figure 1.1 presents an example of a typical distributed enterprise application system, which will be used throughout this thesis and will be referred to as *Running Example 1*. The example system conforms to the common three-tier architectural style of enterprise applications [Fow02]. Each of the tiers comprises a number of instances, to which requests are distributed over load balancers. Each instance comprises a complex stack of software architecture, middleware services, operating system, virtualization, and hardware components.

In this example, it can be observed that at 4:05 PM Quality of Service (QoS) problems manifest themselves at the system boundary as a prompt increase in response times and failing requests for the provided service. Online failure prediction approaches aim to predict failures before they occur in order to allow timely actions, such as preventive maintenance, to decrease or completely prevent system downtime. However, in this case, neither of the two metrics measured at the system boundary gives an indication about the upcoming problem. The traditional approaches for online failure prediction, e.g., time series forecasting based on service response time, are not appropriate in this case because the data does not contain any symptom that precedes the failure.

In addition to the system architecture, Figure 1.1 includes three system-internal measures of the business-tier instance BT2, namely the utilization of CPU, system memory, and heap space of the Java Virtual Machine (JVM). It can be observed that the CPU utilization increases abruptly at 4:05 PM—the same time as the increase of the service response time. The utilization of system memory increases linearly until 3:55 PM when it reaches a level close to 100% and remains stable. The JVM heap space utilization shows an increasing trend until reaching almost 100%. In this scenario, by analyzing the measurements of internal components, we can conclude that the increase of the response times is caused by the increase of the CPU utilization. The increase of the CPU utilization is in turn caused by garbage collection activity inside the JVM—a common problem in Java systems. In this scenario, the

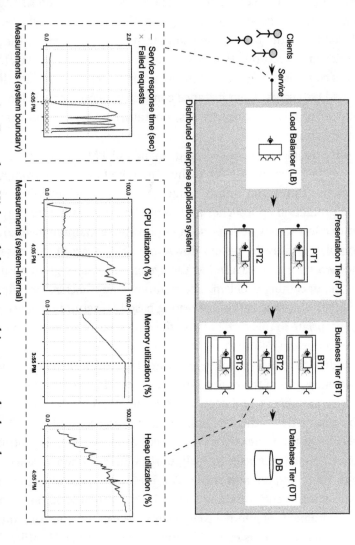

Figure 1.1.: *Running Example 1*: High-level three-tier architecture and selected measurements

root cause of the failure could be a memory leak in the BT2, which causes a chain of errors [Nyg18] that propagates to the end users.

1.3. Overview of Contribution

To overcome the challenges of predicting failures in complex systems, we hypothesize that online failure prediction can be improved by including architectural information of software systems, e.g., how components depend on each other. A complex system is usually composed of many components that work together to deliver the results [BCK12; TMD09]. A failure of one component in the system can cause other components to be unable to complete their tasks. As a consequence, this failure can propagate from one component in the backend of the system to the system boundary and, finally, the users [ANS+04; CG07; HJS01].

In this thesis, we propose an architecture-aware online failure prediction approach, called HORA.[1] The core idea is to first predict the failures of individual components, instead of the whole system. These prediction results are then combined with the architectural knowledge to relate the effects to other components. In the last step, the final failure probabilities are computed to conclude if individual component failures can cause other components or the whole system to fail. Both the prediction of component failures and the architectural knowledge of the system are continuously updated at runtime to reflect the actual state of the system. The HORA approach is divided into three steps which are: (1) component failure prediction, (2) architectural dependency modeling, and (3) failure propagation modeling. Figure 1.2 depicts the high-level architecture and workflow of HORA which will be summarized in more detail in the following subsections.

1.3.1. Component Failure Prediction

The first step of the HORA approach, denoted by (1) in Figure 1.2, focuses on predicting the failure of each component in the system. The prediction

---

[1]Hora is a Thai word meaning "oracle".

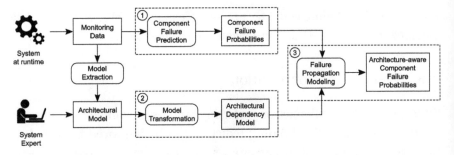

Figure 1.2.: High-level overview of the HORA approach

is made based on the monitoring data obtained at runtime to accurately represent the current status of the components. In contrast to the traditional prediction approaches, which use one monolithic prediction model for the whole system, we aim to predict the failure of individual components as a first step. This approach simplifies the prediction by focusing on a smaller set of data and allowing suitable prediction techniques to be applied for different types of components. Since different types of components provide different types of monitoring data, some prediction techniques are more suitable for some types of data than the others. For example, CPU utilization and method response times are time series data while log files are event-based data. This step investigates the failure prediction based on three types of data, namely, Self-Monitoring, Analysis and Reporting Technology (S.M.A.R.T.) data from hard drives, log files from supercomputers, and time series data from resource utilization and method response times.

1.3.2. Architectural Dependency Modeling

The architecture of a system plays an important role in the propagation of a failure. A failure of one component can affect another if there is a dependency between them. For example, a failure of a database can cause an update method in another component to be unable to complete the request. In this second step of the contribution, we focus on creating a model that can represent the dependencies between components in a system.

The model is able to show the dependencies between components and the dependency weights that indicate how much each component depends on the others. This step is denoted by ② in Figure 1.2.

In this thesis, the dependency model is extracted from a SLAstic architectural model [Hoo14] which is, in turn, extracted from the monitoring data collected by an Application Performance Monitoring (APM) framework, namely, Kieker [HWH12]. The monitoring data can show how a system, including its components, behaves when deployed in a real environment. For instance, a component that makes a lot of calls to another component means that the first is highly dependent on the latter. If the latter fails, it is also likely that the first will also fail. Thus, the monitoring data is obtained from a live system so that the actual behavior of the components is observed.

1.3.3. Failure Propagation Modeling

The last step of the HORA approach, denoted by ③ in Figure 1.2, is combining the results of component failure prediction and architectural dependency modeling. The architectural dependency model in the second step is transformed into a more sophisticated model. The new model employs Bayesian network theory to relate all components in the system through the dependency chain. The results from the component failure prediction are added to the model at regular intervals to reflect the actual status of the components. With these two pieces of information, an inference of the model can be carried out to obtain the predicted effects of the failures, i.e., which components will be affected by the failures of which components and what are the failure probabilities. The results include not only the independent failure probabilities of components, but also the probabilities that they may fail based on the architecture of the system.

1.4. Thesis Structure

This thesis is composed of four main parts. Part I presents foundations and related work. Chapter 2 provides a foundation for proactive fault management, online failure prediction techniques, and architecture-based software QoS management. Chapter 3 presents the existing work related to online failure prediction and architecture-based software QoS prediction by categorizing them into four groups.

Part II presents the contributions of this thesis which is divided into four chapters. Chapter 4 presents the addressed research questions, the research plan, and the overview of the HORA approach. Chapter 5 presents the techniques that are used to predict failures based on three types of data collected from components in software systems, namely, time-series data, event-based data, and S.M.A.R.T. data. Chapter 6 describes the Architectural Dependency Model (ADM), which is an architectural model used to represent component dependency information, and how it is extracted from the existing architectural models. Chapter 7 presents the Failure Propagation Model (FPM), which employs the Bayesian network theory to predict the probability of a component failure causing other components and the whole system to fail. Chapter 8 presents two implementations of the HORA approach.

Part III presents the evaluation of the HORA approach. Chapter 9 presents the evaluation methodology, which includes the overview of the evaluation, the evaluation metrics, and statistical hypothesis testing. The evaluation results of time series-based failure prediction, critical event prediction, and hard drive failure prediction are presented in Chapters 10 to 12, respectively.

Part IV draws the conclusions for the thesis (Chapter 14) and lists the possible future work to improve HORA and online failure prediction (Chapter 15). Additionally, supplementary material, containing software, dataset, and results, is publicly available online [Pit18].

Part I.

Foundations and Related Work

CHAPTER 2

FOUNDATIONS

The HORA approach presented in this thesis employs both online failure prediction and architectural knowledge to predict the failures and their impacts on the system. Online failure prediction is the first step to proactive fault management which aims to handle unexpected events before they cause damage to the system. Architectural knowledge provides the insight into the system regarding how components depend on each other and how a failure of one component can affect the others.

This chapter presents the foundations for the subsequent chapters. Section 2.1 introduces the concepts of proactive fault management and online failure prediction. Section 2.2 presents online failure prediction techniques, which are time series forecasting, machine learning, and pattern recognition, that will be used later in this thesis. Section 2.3 presents architecture-based software performance management approaches which aim at modeling and predicting Quality of Service (QoS) metrics of software systems based on architectural knowledge.

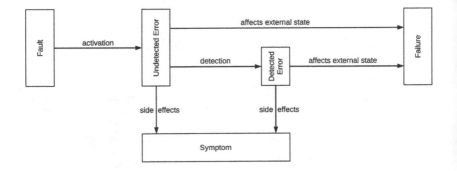

Figure 2.1.: Relationship between fault, symptom, error and failure [SLM10]

2.1. Proactive Fault Management and Online Failure Prediction

This section presents the foundations of proactive fault management. Section 2.1.1 introduces the terminology. Section 2.1.2 presents the steps involved in proactive fault managment. Section 2.1.3 presents online failure prediction, which is the first step to proactive fault management and the main focus of the thesis.

2.1.1. Terminology

Avizienis et al. [ALRL04] provide the basic concepts and taxonomy of dependable and secure computing, which include definitions for failure, errors, and faults. Salfner, Lenk, and Malek [SLM10] further extend these definitions and present five different types of data that are collected at different stages of fault manifestation. Figure 2.1 depicts these five types of data, which are fault, undetected error, detected error, symptom, and failure, and how a fault can manifest itself into a failure that is visible outside the system.

- A *Fault* is the root cause that, when activated, becomes an error and may turn the system into an erroneous state. In the case of a memory leak, the fault is the code in the program that allocates some amount of memory but does not release it after use. If this code is never executed,

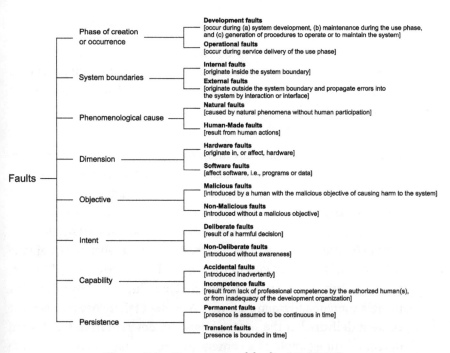

Figure 2.2.: Taxonomy of faults [ALRL04]

it remains dormant and would never cause any errors or, consequently, failures. Avizienis et al. [ALRL04] introduce a taxonomy of faults, as depicted in Figure 2.2, which classifies faults into eight basic view points with two classes of faults in each view point.

- An *Error* is a state of the system when it has deviated from the correct service but the effects are still not observable by the users. For example, when the code that causes a memory leak is executed, the system then turns into an erroneous state. In this state, the program is causing the system to allocate more and more memory but the effect is still not visible from outside. An error can be further categorized into two types, which are *undetected* and *detected errors*. When an error occurs, it remains in the undetected state until it is discovered by inspecting the system, such as checking error messages in the log files. Although an error can be detected, it may still remain invisible from the users.

- A *Symptom* is an observable side effect that results from an erroneous state of the system. An example of a symptom could be a high amount of memory usage caused by a memory leak. As long as the usage is below the available memory, the system may continue to run without any observable problem.

- A *Failure* is an event of a deviation of the system from a correct service. The event is observable outside the system boundary by its users or third-party systems. A failure does not necessarily have to be a total outage and can be defined in different ways depending on the requirements of the service. For example, a slow response time or a certain failure rate can also be regarded as failures when the Quality of Service (QoS) requirements or the Service Level Objectives (SLOs) are violated. Avizienis et al. [ALRL04] divide failures into two domains, namely content and timing failures. A content failure occurs when the content delivered at the service boundary deviates from the desired outcome. An example of a content failure is a fault in an algorithm that causes the computation to deliver an incorrect result. A timing failure occurs when the time that the service is delivered deviates from the intended time. An example of a timing failure is an airbag in a car that inflates before or after when it is intended to.

2.1.2. Proactive Fault Management

Proactive fault management is an approach that aims to proactively handle failures in the system so that it can continue to provide the intended operation in unexpected events [SLM10]. The idea originates from the attempt to improve the QoS of information systems despite the increasing complexity. A number of approaches have been proposed and actively researched, such as self-aware, self-configuring, and self-healing systems, including proactive fault management [BJM+05].

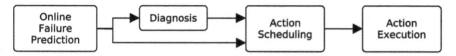

Figure 2.3.: Steps involved in proactive fault management [SLM10]

Avizienis et al. [ALRL04] group means to attain dependability and security into the four following major categories.

- *Fault prevention* aims to prevent the introduction of faults in the system.

- *Fault tolerance* aims to prevent the system from failing in the presence of faults.

- *Fault removal* aims to reduce the number of faults and their severity.

- *Fault forecasting* aims to estimate the number of faults in the system, predict future incidence and consequences of faults.

Among these four categories, fault prevention, fault removal, and a part of fault forecasting aim at attaining system dependability during the development phase. On the other hand, fault tolerance and a part of fault forecasting aim at attaining system dependability when faults are triggered at runtime and have a tendency of leading to a failure.

In contrast to other means, proactive fault management, which falls into the fault forecasting category, aims to prevent the faults that exist in the system at runtime from being activated and leading to a failure. However, if the failure cannot be completely prevented, its consequences should be mitigated, i.e., there should be as little effect as possible on other parts of the system. In order to achieve this goal, the four following steps are involved in proactive fault management [SLM10]. These steps are depicted in Figure 2.3.

1. *Online failure prediction* is the first step to proactive fault management. The goal is to predict the upcoming problems that can cause a component or a system to fail in the very near future. It takes runtime monitoring data as input so that the predictions are made based on

the current state of the system. The prediction result can be in either a binary form, which indicates whether the system is going to fail, or a continuous value, which represents how likely the system is going to fail.

2. *Diagnosis* is optionally performed in order to obtain more information regarding the problems so that the action can be planned accordingly. For some recovery actions, it is sufficient to know the coarse location of the failure. For example, if an instance of a microservice is predicted to fail, a new instance can be spawned to replace the failing one. However, further information may be required to pinpoint the exact location of the fault that causes the failure. In this case, a fault localization technique can be applied to find the location of the root cause. Another example of the diagnosis step is deciding which countermeasure is suitable to prevent the problem or mitigate its effects so that the operation of the system is disturbed as little as possible.

3. *Action scheduling* is performed to determine when would be the best time to apply the selected countermeasure. This step needs to consider the results from the online failure prediction and diagnosis steps. The result of the online failure prediction tells how likely it is that the failure will occur, how severe it would be, and when the expected time of occurrence is. The result of the diagnosis tells what needs to be done to the system to prevent the upcoming problem. For example, for a web service that is predicted to fail in a few days, the countermeasure, e.g., a reboot, can be scheduled at night when the workload is low. For a system that is predicted to fail very soon, the countermeasure might be executed immediately to prevent further damage caused by a system failure.

4. *Action execution* performs the planned countermeasure. This step requires the action to be done while maintaining the integrity of the system, such as data synchronization or keeping the existing sessions alive.

Online failure prediction is one of the most important steps of proactive fault management. Accurate predictions allow the other three steps to be carried out efficiently while wrong predictions can cause unnecessary actions or insufficient preparations. For example, a false positive may trigger cold backup instances to warm up. On the other hand, a false negative would not trigger any action resulting in an unexpected failure.

The remainder of this thesis focuses on online failure prediction and introduces an approach to improve the prediction quality. Thus, the diagnosis, action scheduling, and action execution steps will not be covered in this thesis.

2.1.3. Online Failure Prediction

The goal of online failure prediction is to predict upcoming failures in a system before they occur [SLM10]. The prediction allows the operators to diagnose the system and to find a solution to prevent the problem from occurring or to minimize the impact on the system. Many prediction techniques can be employed depending on the types of available input data.

Figure 2.4 depicts the timeline of online failure prediction. The *observation window* Δt_d is the period in which the data is observed from the system. During this period various parameters are monitored, e.g., log files, resource utilization, or failure events. The *lead time* Δt_l is the time between when the prediction result is obtained and the expected time of failure occurrence. The *minimum warning time* Δt_w is the minimum period which is needed for preparing the countermeasure. For example, warming up spare units would take time until they are ready to replace the failing ones. If a prediction is made after this point, there will not be enough time to prevent the problem from occurring. The *prediction period* Δt_p is the expected time that the predicted failure will occur. A small prediction period allows countermeasures to be scheduled and executed effectively. However, predicting the exact time of a failure is not a trivial task. On the other hand, a large prediction period is not very useful since the exact time of the failure is not known.

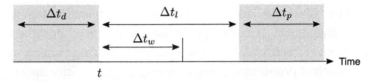

Figure 2.4.: Timeline of online failure prediction [SLM10]

2.2. Online Failure Prediction Techniques

This section introduces techniques that will be used to predict component failures in Chapter 5. Section 2.2.1 presents time series forecasting techniques. Section 2.2.2 presents machine learning and pattern recognition techniques. Section 2.2.3 introduces the formalism of Bayesian network which is the core of the Failure Propagation Model (FPM) of HORA.

2.2.1. Time Series-based Failure Prediction Techniques

Time series data is a sequence of random variables that are taken or observed at regular intervals [SS11]. The resulting data points are usually equally spaced in time and ordered by the time they are collected. A time series data X can be formally represented as

$$X = \{x_1, x_2, \ldots, x_t\} \tag{2.1}$$

where $t \in \mathbb{Z}$ and x_i is an observed random variable with $1 \leq i \leq t$. Examples of this type of data are average temperature over time, sampled sound wave, stock market. In computer systems, time series data can be, for instance, load average, CPU temperature, or memory utilization that are collected at regular intervals, e.g., every second, by the operating system. Another example is the service response time that is collected and aggregated to provide measurements at regular intervals.

One important property of time series data is stationarity. A time series data is strictly stationary if the probabilistic behaviors at any time points are

| Data collection | Model training | Forecast |

Figure 2.5.: Workflow of time series forecasting

identical [SS11]. This can be expressed as

$$P\{x_s \leq c\} = P\{x_t \leq c\} \tag{2.2}$$

where $s, t \in \mathbb{Z}$ and $s \neq t$. This property means that the mean value at time s, μ_s, is equal to the mean value at time t, μ_t. However, this property is hard to prove for a single data set. Thus, a definition for weakly stationary time series is defined as [SS11]

1. the mean value function is constant and does not depend on time

2. the autocovariance function depends on s and t only through their difference.

The goal of time series forecasting is to predict the future value of a series based on the past values. For online failure prediction, one is interested in knowing if the future value will exceed a predefined threshold or violate the SLOs. Figure 2.5 depicts the workflow of the prediction. The input is the time series data collected from the components in the system. The forecasting algorithm uses the historical data to create a model that can best describe the characteristics of the data. The model is then used to forecast the future value of the data. If the forecasted value exceeds the predefined threshold, a violation, which can lead to a failure, can be expected. On the system level, an SLO violation can be an increasing response time of the service over a certain value or decreasing availability of the service. On the component level, a threshold violation can be an over-utilization of the CPU, memory, or network, or an increase in the method response time, which can cause that component to fail or unable to process the requests. This section presents selected time series forecasting techniques that can be used to predict future values of time series data.

2.2.1.1. Mean

Time series forecasting using mean values makes an assumption that the probabilistic behavior of the data in the future remains the same. Thus, the future value is the mean value of the historical data points. The mean value can be expressed as

$$x_t = \frac{x_{t-1} + x_{t-2} + \cdots + x_{t-n}}{n} = \frac{1}{n}\sum_{i=1}^{n} x_i \tag{2.3}$$

where n is the number of past values to be considered.

2.2.1.2. Last

Time series forecasting using the last value is a straightforward and simple way of prediction. It is based on an assumption that the values of two consecutive data points are close to each other. Therefore, the last observed value is used as the predicted value.

$$x_t = x_{t-1} \tag{2.4}$$

2.2.1.3. Autoregressive Moving Average

Autoregressive Moving Average (ARMA) is a model which is composed of two parts; autoregression and moving average. The autoregressive model uses a function of the past values $x_{t-1}, x_{t-2}, ..., x_{t-p}$ to forecast the current value x_t. The order p determines the number of past value considered in the model. An autoregressive model of order p, which can be written as **AR**(p), can be expressed as [SS11]

$$x_t = \phi_1 x_{t-1} + \phi_2 x_{t-2} + \ldots + \phi_p x_{t-p} + \omega_t \qquad (2.5)$$

where $\phi_1, \phi_2, \ldots, \phi_p$ are constants with $\phi_p \neq 0$, and ω_t is white Gaussian noise with $\mu_\omega = 0$ and $\sigma_\omega^2 = 1$. If the mean of x_t is not zero, the expression becomes

$$x_t - \mu = \phi_1(x_{t-1} - \mu) + \phi_2(x_{t-2} - \mu) + \ldots + \phi_p(x_{t-p} - \mu) + \omega_t \qquad (2.6)$$

$$x_t = \alpha + \phi_1 x_{t-1} + \phi_2 x_{t-2} + \ldots + \phi_p x_{t-p} + \omega_t \qquad (2.7)$$

where $\alpha = \mu(1 - \phi_1 - \phi_2 - \ldots - \phi_p)$.

A moving average model of order q, written as **MA**(q), uses a function of the past values of white noise [SS11]. The model can be expressed as

$$x_t = \omega_t + \theta_1 \omega_{t-1} + \theta_2 \omega_{t-2} + \ldots + \theta_q \omega_{t-q} \qquad (2.8)$$

where $\theta_1, \theta_2, \ldots, \theta_q$ are parameters with $\theta_q \neq 0$ and ω_t is a Gaussian white noise series with $\mu = 0$.

The autoregressive and moving average can be combined into one ARMA model which is expressed as

$$x_t = \phi_1 x_{t-1} + \phi_2 x_{t-2} + \ldots + \phi_p x_{t-p} + \omega_t +$$
$$\theta_1 \omega_{t-1} + \theta_2 \omega_{t-2} + \ldots + \theta_q \omega_{t-q} \qquad (2.9)$$

The model becomes an autoregressive model when $q = 0$ and a moving average model when $p = 0$.

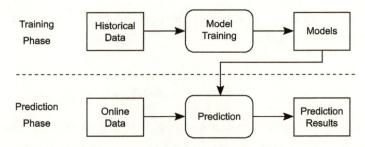

Figure 2.6.: Workflow of machine learning

2.2.1.4. Autoregressive Integrated Moving Average

The ARMA model described previously assumes that the time series data is stationary. Differencing can be applied to the data in order to make it stationary as follows [SS11].

$$\nabla x_t = x_t - x_{t-1} \tag{2.10}$$

The order of the differencing defines how many times it is applied to the data. This step can be included in the ARMA which results in an Autoregressive Integrated Moving Average (ARIMA) model.

2.2.2. Machine Learning and Pattern Recognition

Machine learning algorithms have been widely used in various fields of research and have shown good performance in learning and recognizing patterns [Bis06]. In online failure prediction, we make an assumption that there is observable data, i.e., symptoms and detected errors, that usually precede the failures [SLM10]. If we are able to detect them at runtime, we will also be able to tell if a failure is likely to occur in the near future.

Figure 2.6 depicts the process of using machine learning algorithms to predict failures. During the training phase, the data is collected from the system and analyzed by the learning algorithms. The algorithms create the models that can represent the system in different states. For example, one model may represent the state in which the system is functioning correctly while another model may represent the system in a faulty state. At runtime, the data is collected from the running system and analyzed. If the pattern of the data matches the pattern of one of the models, the system is classified to be in the state that the model represents.

Based on the data available during the training phase, machine learning and pattern recognition techniques can be further categorized into the three following groups [HTF01].

- *Supervised learning.* The techniques in this category learn the models from a set of labeled data. Specifically, the input data used in the learning phase is labeled with the desired outputs. The data is usually labeled by experts who manually assign the desired output to each data point. The task of the algorithm is to find a way to differentiate these data points. An example of supervised learning is Optical Character Recognition (OCR), which is used to recognize images of characters or digitize physical books into a digital format. The algorithm is trained by learning from images of characters and creating the corresponding models for the characters.

- *Unsupervised learning.* The techniques in this category learn the models from unlabeled data. The goal of the algorithm is to classify similar data points into groups by discovering the patterns in the data. In contrast to supervised learning, there is no correct answer in unsupervised learning. An example of unsupervised learning is classifying customers of an online shopping website into groups based on their behaviors.

- *Semi-supervised learning.* Semi-supervised learning learns the models from partially labeled data. This method reduces the effort of labeling the data in supervised learning while providing more control of the output than unsupervised learning. An example of semi-supervised learning is anomaly detection. The algorithm is trained with sets of data that represent normal states. When the algorithm finds a data point that does not belong to any of the model, it is then classified as anomalous.

In this section, we classify machine learning techniques into six categories based on the underlying concepts. The techniques in each category can be either supervised, semi-supervised, or unsupervised learning. These techniques will be used in Chapter 5 to predict component failures based on event logs and Self-Monitoring, Analysis and Reporting Technology (S.M.A.R.T.) data.

2.2.2.1. Probabilistic Models

Probabilistic models are based on a concept that there are uncertainties in the future events. In order to build models that can represent the uncertainties, they analyze probability distributions of random variables in the dataset. At runtime, the observed variables are fed to the models which give probabilities of the variables of interest as output.

- Naïve Bayes Classifier (NBC) is a simple but powerful learning algorithm based on Bayes' theorem [LD05]. The learning phase analyzes the dataset and builds probability distribution models of the attributes. When the models are obtained, the prediction is carried out by calculating the probability of all attributes under the assumption that all attributes are independent and identically distributed.

- Multinomial Naïve Bayes Classifier (MNBC) is another application of the Bayes' theorem, which uses multinomial distributions as the underlying model instead of normal distributions. This technique allows the count of the occurrences for each value to be integrated into the model and has been successfully used in areas such as text classification (e.g., [KFPH05]).

- Bayesian Network (BN) is a directed acyclic graph that represents the conditional probability between each attribute [FGG97]. The construction of the network comprises two steps: building the structure of the network and estimating the probabilities. During runtime, the joint probability of an instance belonging to a class is calculated.

2.2.2.2. Decision trees

Decision trees are tree-like graphs. Each node in the graph contains a conditional statement that further splits the node into branches. The classification is represented by the path from the root node to the leaf node.

- C4.5 is a top-down decision tree, introduced by Quinlan [Qui93], that employs a greedy algorithm to find the most important attribute at each step. At each level, the node is split until a leaf containing only instances from one class is achieved.

- Reduced Error Pruning Tree (REPTree) constructs a decision tree by considering the information gain of all attributes in the dataset and splitting a node into further nodes. After the tree is built, the algorithm reduces the overfitting problem by using reduced-error pruning.

- Random Forest (RF) is a collection of decision trees proposed by Breiman [Bre01]. This technique can be viewed as meta-learning [VD02], which improves the prediction quality by casting votes among the trees and assigning the most voted class to the predicted instance.

2.2.2.3. Rule-Based Algorithms

Rule-based algorithms are based on a certain rule or a set of rules. These rules are constructed by analyzing some characteristic or statistics of the training data.

- ZeroR is the simplest classifier that is used to estimate the baseline for machine learning algorithms. The classification is done by classifying all instances as the majority class of the training set.

- OneR denotes a one-rule algorithm introduced by Holte [Hol93] that employs only one rule to classify instances. This rule is constructed by building one rule for each attribute of the dataset and comparing their error rates. The rule of the attribute with the lowest error rate is chosen as the final rule and used in the classification.

- Decision Table (DT), proposed by Kohavi [Koh95], is a table containing a list of training instances with selected attributes. During the classification, an instance is compared to those in the list. If there is a match, it returns the majority class of those matched; otherwise, it returns the majority class of the whole list.

- Repeated Incremental Pruning to Produce Error Reduction (RIPPER), proposed by Cohen [Coh95], builds rules by starting from an empty rule set and adding more rules until all positive instances are added.

- PART is a learning algorithm introduced by Frank and Witten [FW98]. The algorithm employs a divide-and-conquer approach to build the rule set. In each step, a partial decision tree is constructed and a rule is derived from the leaf of the tree that has the highest coverage. The whole process is repeated until the rule set covers all training instances.

2.2.2.4. Hyperplane Separation

Hyperplane separation employs a hyperplane in the multi-dimensional space of the dataset to separate all instances into classes. The goal is to find the plane that provides the maximum separation between each class.

- Support Vector Machine (SVM), introduced by Cortes and Vapnik [CV95], is a technique that separates instances into two distinct classes by drawing a hyperplane between them. When working with a multiple-class classification problem, Support Vector Machine (SVM) classifies instances into one of the two main classes and further splits each class into smaller ones until the final class is obtained.

- Sequential Minimal Optimization (SMO), proposed by Platt [Pla99], is an improvement technique for SVM to speed up the training phase. SMO reduces the internal computation of quadratic problems into smaller sub-problems that can be solved analytically.

- Stochastic Gradient Descent (SGD) is a stochastic optimization algorithm used to solve linear problems [Bot10]. In our experiment, the algorithm is used to build a linear model for SVM during the training phase.

2.2.2.5. Function Approximation

Function approximation estimates functions that map input vectors, which are extracted from an instance, to a value that represents an output class.

- Simple Logistic Regression (SLR) is a linear regression technique that can be used to predict binary-class instances [LHF05]. The algorithm uses LogitBoost [FHT00] to build the regression model and was further improved by Sumner, Frank, and Hall [SFH05] to increase the speed of the model construction.

- Logistic Regression (LR) is similar to simple logistic regression but employs ridge estimators proposed by le Cessie and van Houwelingen [CH92] to reduce the error made by parameter estimation.

- Multilayer Perceptron (MP) is a type of neural network that contains multiple layers of neurons [Hay99]. Each neuron holds a function that maps an input variable to an output variable. The neurons between layers are connected through weighted links, and the final output of the whole network designates the class of the instance.

- Voted Perceptron (VP), introduced by Freund and Schapire [FS98], is a classifier which finds the vector that can linearly separate data into classes, provided that the margin between them is sufficiently large. The performance of this method is claimed to be close to that of SVM but with a faster training time.

2.2.2.6. Instance-based Learning

Instance-based learning or lazy learning [AKA91] is the technique that stores the instances learned during the training phase and postpones any processing or computation until runtime when new instances need to be classified.

- Nearest Neighbor Classifier (NNC) compares a new instance with those stored in the reference set. The new instance and the closest one in the reference set are assumed to be generated from the same class, which is the class assigned to the new instance. Euclidean distance is a function generally used to compute the distance between instances.

- K-Star, introduced by Cleary and Trigg [CT95], is a learning algorithm similar to nearest neighbor classifier. However, the measure for the similarity between the new instance and the references is calculated using an entropy function.

- Locally Weighted Learning (LWL) classifies a new instance based on the weighted distance of the nearest neighbors [AMS97]. Specifically, the underlying algorithm builds naïve Bayes models based on the k-nearest neighbors of the new instance and use these models to compute a class probability of that instance [FHP03].

2.2.3. Bayesian Network

In order to model the failure propagation between components in the system, a model that can represent the components and their dependencies is required. This section focuses on Bayesian network which is used by HORA to represent this information.

A Bayesian network is a Directed Acyclic Graph (DAG) that represents conditional probabilities between random variables [Bis06]. The vertices in the graph represent random variables, while the edges represent conditional probabilities between those variables. A common use case of a Bayesian network is to represent conditional relationships between events. For example, in the medical domain, it can be used to model the relationships between symptoms and diseases. By observing the presence of symptoms, the probability of having certain diseases can be computed.

Figure 2.7 illustrates a small example of a Bayesian network. The network is composed of three random variables, namely, x_1, x_2, and x_3. The conditional probabilities represented by the edges are x_1 to x_2, x_2 to x_3,

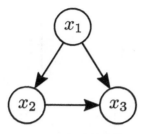

Figure 2.7.: An example of a Bayesian network with three random variables

and x_1 to x_3. By observing the structure of the network, we can see that there are three conditional relationships between x_1, x_2, and x_3. Specifically, x_1 has a direct effect on x_2 and x_3 while x_2 has a direct effect only on x_3. Using Bayes' theorem, these conditional relationships can be mathematically expressed as a joint probability function of the variables, $P(x_1, x_2, x_3)$, which be can written as

$$
\begin{aligned}
P(x_1, x_2, x_3) &= P(x_3|x_1, x_2)P(x_1, x_2) & (2.11)\\
&= P(x_3|x_1, x_2)P(x_2|x_1)P(x_1) & (2.12)
\end{aligned}
$$

The joint probability function comprises three terms, which are $P(x_3|x_1, x_2)$, $P(x_2|x_1)$, and $P(x_1)$. This implies that the probability of x_3 depends on x_1 and x_2. The probability of x_2 depends only on x_1. Lastly, the probability of x_1 does not depend on any other variable. For a Bayesian network with n random variables, $x_1, x_2, \ldots, x_n$, the joint probability function becomes

$$
\begin{aligned}
P(x_1, x_2, \ldots, x_n) &= P(x_n|x_1, x_2, \ldots, x_{n-1})\ldots P(x_2|x_1)P(x_1) & (2.13)\\
&= \prod_{k=1}^{n} P(x_k|\mathrm{pa}_k) & (2.14)
\end{aligned}
$$

where pa_k is the set of parent nodes of x_k.

x_1	
True	False
0.7	0.3

(a) x_1

x_1	x_2	
	True	False
False	0.2	0.8
True	0.8	0.2

(b) x_2

x_1	x_2	x_3	
		True	False
False	False	0.1	0.9
False	True	0.8	0.2
True	False	0.8	0.2
True	True	0.9	0.1

(c) x_3

Table 2.1.: Condition Probability Tables (CPTs) of Bayesian network in Figure 2.7

The joint probability can be computed using the conditional probability between variables. For example, the conditional probability of x_1 and x_2, $P(x_1|x_2)$, is defined as

$$P(x_1|x_2) = \frac{P(x_1 \cap x_2)}{P(x_2)} \tag{2.15}$$

which represents the probability of x_1 given x_2.

The conditional probabilities of the variables in the Bayesian network can be represented in a table form which is called Condition Probability Table (CPT). Each node in the network has one table associated with it. Table 2.1 illustrates an example of three tables corresponding to the three variables of the network in Figure 2.7. Each table lists the probability of the variable given all conditions of the dependent variables. In this example, we assume that a variable can be either *true* or *false*. For instance, the CPT of x_1, which does not depend on other variables, contains only one row. This means that the probability of x_1 is not influenced by other variables. The CPT of x_2, which depends on x_1, contains one additional row for x_1. The probability of x_2 is, thus, influenced by x_1. The CPT of x_3 contains two additional rows as it depends on both x_1 and x_2.

The probability of an event occurring can be computed using the joint probability function and the CPTs. For example, the probability of x_1, x_2, and x_3 being true can be computed as

$$P(x_3 = T, x_1 = T, x_2 = T) = P(x_3 = T \mid x_1 = T, x_2 = T)$$
$$P(x_2 = T \mid x_1 = T)P(x_1 = T) \quad (2.16)$$

By substituting the probabilities from Table 2.1, we obtain

$$P(x_3 = T, x_1 = T, x_2 = T) \quad = \quad 0.9 \times 0.8 \times 0.7 \quad (2.17)$$
$$= \quad 0.504 \quad (2.18)$$

Another application of Bayesian networks is for inferring probability of unobserved random variables. For example, if x_1 and x_2 can not be observed and we would like to know the probability of x_3 being true, the equation becomes

$$P(x_3 = T) \quad = \quad \sum_{x_1, x_2 \in \{T,F\}} P(x_3 = T, x_1, x_2) \quad (2.19)$$

However, if x_1 is observed to be true, the probability of x_3 being true given that x_1 is true can be computed as

$$P(x_3 = T \mid x_1 = T) = \frac{P(x_1 = T, x_3 = T)}{P(x_1 = T)} \quad (2.20)$$
$$= \frac{\sum_{x_2 \in \{T,F\}} P(x_1 = T, x_2, x_3 = T)}{\sum_{x_2, x_3 \in \{T,F\}} P(x_1 = T, x_2, x_3)} \quad (2.21)$$

The numerator of Equation 2.21 can be expanded and computed as follows.

$$\sum_{x_2 \in \{T,F\}} P(x_1 = T, x_2, x_3 = T) = P(x_1 = T, x_2 = T, x_3 = T)$$

$$+ P(x_1 = T, x_2 = F, x_3 = T) \qquad (2.22)$$

$$= \{P(x_3 = T|x_1 = T, x_2 = T)$$

$$P(x_2 = T|x_1 = T)P(x_1 = T)\} +$$

$$\{P(x_3 = T|x_1 = T, x_2 = F)$$

$$P(x_2 = F|x_1 = T)P(x_1 = T)\} \qquad (2.23)$$

$$= (0.9 \times 0.8 \times 0.7) +$$

$$(0.8 \times 0.2 \times 0.7) \qquad (2.24)$$

$$= 0.504 + 0.112 \qquad (2.25)$$

$$= 0.616 \qquad (2.26)$$

Similarly, the denominator of Equation 2.21 can be expanded and computed as follows.

$$\sum_{x_2, x_3 \in \{T,F\}} P(x_1 = T, x_2, x_3) = P(x_1 = T, x_2 = T, x_3 = T) +$$

$$P(x_1 = T, x_2 = T, x_3 = F) +$$

$$P(x_1 = T, x_2 = F, x_3 = T) +$$

$$P(x_1 = T, x_2 = F, x_3 = F) \qquad (2.27)$$

$$= 0.504 + 0.056 + 0.112 + 0.028 \qquad (2.28)$$

$$= 0.7 \qquad (2.29)$$

By substituting the numerator and denominator of Equation 2.21, we obtain

$$P(x_3 = T|x_1 = T) = \frac{0.616}{0.7} \qquad (2.30)$$

$$= 0.88 \qquad (2.31)$$

2.3. Architecture-based Software Quality of Service Management

The HORA approach introduced in this thesis employs an architectural model to capture the dependencies between components and combines it with the monitoring data obtained at runtime to improve the failure prediction. This section introduces the relevant foundations on architecture-based QoS management approaches. Section 2.3.1 provides the basic concept of architecture and the definitions. Section 2.3.2 describes Architecture Description Languages (ADLs) which are notations for modeling software architecture. Section 2.3.3 introduces model-based software QoS evaluation that employs models to evaluate different aspects of a system. Section 2.3.4 presents Application Performance Monitoring (APM) which monitors the system at runtime and uses the data to improve system performance. Section 2.3.5 presents the SLAstic approach, the SLAstic model, and Kieker, which are used by HORA to represent architecture knowledge and to monitor the system.

2.3.1. Software Architecture

Taylor, Medvidović, and Dashofy [TMD09] define a software architecture as the set of principal design decisions made about the system during the development and its evolution. These design decisions characterize the system and describe various aspects, e.g., structure, behavior, interaction, nonfunctional properties, and implementation. ISO/IEC/IEEE 42010:2011(E) [ISO11] provides another definition of a system architecture as follows, which will be used in this thesis.

Definition 2.1 ((System) Architecture [ISO11])
Fundamental concepts or properties of a system in its environment embodied in its elements, relationships, and in the principles of its design and evolution.

In this section, basic terminology related to architecture, which are component, connector, configuration, and style will be introduced.

2.3.1.1. Component

A software component is an entity that provides functionalities required by the system or other components. Taylor, Medvidović, and Dashofy [TMD09] define a software component as follows.

Definition 2.2 (Software component [TMD09])
A software component is an architectural entity that (1) encapsulates a subset of the system's functionality and/or data, (2) restricts access to that subset via an explicity defined interface, and (3) has explicitly defined dependencies on its required execution context.

In other words, a component encompasses the state, which is represented in a form of information or data, and the functionalities, which is provided by its interface. A component may require other components to function, which is regarded as execution context. These components can be hardware or software resources, configurations, data, or other components that provides functionalities required by this component.

Szyperski [Szy02] provides another definition for a software component from another perspective.

Definition 2.3 (Software component [Szy02])
A software component is a unit of composition with contractually specified interfaces and explicit context dependencies only. A software component can be deployed independently and is subject to composition by third parties.

This definition implies that a software component can be reused in another system if both systems require the same functionalities provided by that component. For example, the Apache commons mathematics library[1] is a light-weight software library that provides mathematics and statistics functionalities. The library is widely used because it provides common functionalities required by most applications.

---

[1] http://commons.apache.org/proper/commons-math/

In order for software components to function, they need to be deployed on hardware components. IEEE 610.10-1994 [IEE95] provides a definition for hardware as follows.

Definition 2.4 (Hardware [IEE95])
Physical equipment used to process, store, or transmit computer programs or data.

In *Running Example 1*, software components are, for example, web applications, application server, and Database Management System (DBMS). Example of hardware components are the physical components, e.g., CPU, memory, and hard drives.

2.3.1.2. Connector

Connectors provide interactions between components so that they can communicate and work together. Taylor, Medvidović, and Dashofy [TMD09] provide a definition for software connector as follows.

Definition 2.5 (Software connector [TMD09])
"A software connector is an architectural element tasked with effecting and regulating interactions among components."

In a monolithic application, software connectors are, for example, procedural calls or shared data access. A procedural call provides communications by transferring control and data between program subroutines. The caller passes control to the callee by invocation with parameters and the callee returns the control with the return value to the caller. A shared data access provides interactions between components by making certain data accessible for multiple components. In a more complex distributed application, which involves components that are deployed on multiple machines in different locations, connectors are usually Application Programming Interfaces (APIs) that allow components to interact remotely.

As opposed to software connectors, hardware connectors are physical entities that connect and provide communication between physical components.

An example of a hardware connector is physical network links that connect multiple machines.

In *Running Example 1*, software connectors are entities that provide (remote) procedural calls, while hardware connectors are network connections between physical machines.

2.3.1.3. Configuration

When building a system, components and connectors need to be put together in a certain way which is called a configuration. Taylor, Medvidović, and Dashofy [TMD09] define a configuration as follows.

Definition 2.6 (Configuration [TMD09])
An architectural configuration is a set of specific associations between the components and connectors of a software system's architecture.

An architectural configuration can be represented in a form of a diagram or a graph. The nodes in the graph are components while the edges represent connectors. A connection between components implies that those components can interact and communicate with each other.

An architectural configuration also creates an architectural dependency. When two components are connected, an architectural dependency emerges from the connection. Stafford, Wolf, and Caporuscio [SWC03] classify architectural dependencies into two categories, namely structure and behavior. Structural dependencies come from system dependencies, e.g., import statements, and deployment of software components on hardware components. Behavioral dependencies come from dynamic interactions between components.

Figure 1.1 (Page 4) depicts a configuration of *Running Example 1* as a diagram. The diagram shows how software components are deployed and how hardware components are connected. The dependencies between both software and hardware components are also visible.

2.3.1.4. Architectural Style

There are certain design decisions that result in a system with better properties than the others. These decisions are generally at high-level and are not specific to one particular system. Examples of architectural styles are client-server, pipe-and-filter, Representational State Transfer (REST), component-based, Service-oriented Architecture (SOA), and microservice [New15]. Taylor, Medvidović, and Dashofy [TMD09] provide a definition for an architectural style as follows.

Definition 2.7 (Architectural style [TMD09])
An architectural style is a named collection of architectural design decisions that (1) are applicable in a given development context, (2) constrain architectural design decisions that are specific to a particular system within that context, and (3) elicit beneficial qualities in each resulting system.

Running Example 1 in Figure 1.1 (Page 4) follows a three-tier architectural style since the system is split into three parts, namely presentation tier, business tier, and database tier.

2.3.2. Architecture Description Language

Architecture Description Languages (ADLs) are notations that are developed particularly for modeling software architecture [TMD09]. ISO/IEC/IEEE 42010:2011(E) [ISO11] defines an Architecture Description Language (ADL) as follows.

Definition 2.8 (Architecture Description Language [ISO11])
An Architecture Description Language (ADL) is any form of expression for use in architecture descriptions.

Medvidović and Taylor [MT00] conducted a survey on the existing ADLs and found a key property among them which is the support for modeling component, connectors, interfaces, and configurations. Examples of early ADLs are Darwin, Rapide, and Wright, which were developed primarily for research projects and are no longer actively used in practice [TMD09].

Besides, there are domain-specific ADLs, for example, Architecture Analysis and Design Language (AADL) [FGH06], which is developed for modeling real-time and embedded systems, e.g., automotive, avionics, and medical systems. Additionally, there are extensible ADLs, for example, Acme [GMW10], which provide basic constructs and allow modifications or creation of new constructs.

2.3.3. Model-based Software Quality of Service Evaluation

Early evaluation of the system attributes based on a prototype can provide insights of the system without having to build a real system. For example, aerospace engineers use a model of a plane to test its aerodynamics in a wind tunnel before it is built. Moreover, with the help of computers, the aerodynamics can nowadays be simulated in a virtual environment.

In software engineering, the design decisions made in the early stage of development can affect non-functional properties of the system, e.g., performance, availability, reliability, scalability, cost efficiency, or energy efficiency. Such aspects can be evaluated by using a measurement-based evaluation which deploys the system in an environment that is identical or similar to the production system and observes those aspects. For example, performance characteristics of a system can be measured and used to improve the QoS, for example, see [AGK+02; MA01]. However, this approach requires a lot of effort in setting up the environment and deploying the system. Furthermore, for some of the aspects, more effort would be needed, for example, the system needs to be actually scaled to evaluate its scalability.

Model-based software QoS evaluation allows such aspects to be analyzed or evaluated without actually deploying the system or even before the software is fully developed. This enables design alternatives to be considered and evaluated in order to meet the non-functional requirements. Moreover, any changes made to the architecture during the evolution can be analyzed to see if they will affect non-functional properties of the system.

There exist two approaches for model-based software QoS evaluation. The first approach employs analytical models while the second approach employs architecture-level models [BHW+15]. Analytical models are primarily based on mathematical models, such as queueing networks, layered queueing networks, Petri nets, reliability block diagrams, and fault trees [ACC+14]. The models can be evaluated by the suitable model solvers to obtain the desired QoS value. For instance, a reliability block diagram can be solved by RBDTool [SRSD04] to obtain system reliability and a fault tree can be solved by OpenFTA[1] to obtain failure probability.

Architecture-level models are based on the system architecture, including the deployment and available resources. One example of such models is Schedulability, Performance and Time Specification (SPT) [Obj05] which is an Object Management Group (OMG) standard for modeling system performance using Unified Modeling Language (UML). Modeling and Analysis of Real Time and Embedded systems (MARTE) [Obj11] is another OMG standard for modeling real-time and embedded systems. The standard utilizes Unified Modeling Language 2 (UML2) which has been extended to support model-driven development of such systems. A more sophisticated example is the Palladio Component Model (PCM) which allows an evaluation of various QoS aspects, such as performance, reliability, maintainability, and cost, based on architectural specifications [BKR09]. The Descartes Modeling Language (DML) provides meta-models for modeling QoS aspects, e.g., performance and dependability, and ensuring that these requirements are met during the operation [KBH14]. An architecture-level model can be solved either by simulation using the provided simulators to obtain the properties of interest, or it can be transformed into an analytical model, e.g., Layered Queueing Networks (LQNs) for performance prediction or Markov chains for reliability prediction, and solved using a respective model solver.

2.3.4. Application Performance Management

Hora employs Application Performance Monitoring (APM) to obtain monitoring data of components in the system. The data is used to create models that represent the statuses, e.g., healthy or failing, of the components. At

---

[1]http://www.openfta.com/

runtime, the failure probabilities of the components are predicted by these models and are forwarded to the Failure Propagation Model (FPM) for further inference. This section presents APM and the activities that are involved in the process.

Application Performance Monitoring (APM) aims to achieve a satisfactory level of performance during operation by continuously monitoring relevant parameters, detecting, diagnosing, and resolving problems using the collected data [HHMO17]. Examples of commercial APM tools are Dynatrace,[1] New Relic,[2] AppDynamics,[3] and CA.[4] Examples of open-source tools are Kieker[5] and inspectIT.[6]

Heger et al. [HHMO17] classify APM activities into four groups, which are data collection, data storage and processing, data presentation, and data interpretation and use. For the first activity, the data is collected at runtime from different sources. These sources are further categorized into six levels, which are hardware, operating system, middleware, application, user, and business [HHMO17]. For example, resource utilization can be collected from CPU, memory, disk, or network. Method response times can be collected from internal or remote calls. Conversion and bounce rate can be collected from the business level. Application call stacks can be sampled to obtain the call graph.

In the second activity, the collected monitoring data from the first activity can be stored locally, e.g., in a log file or a local database, or remotely, e.g., a centralized storage system offered by the APM tool. There are two common types of collected data, namely, time series data and execution traces [HHMO17]. Time series data, as defined in Section 2.2.1, usually represents statistics, such as mean or percentile, of the metrics, e.g., method response times and resource utilization. Execution traces represent the control flow of the application and the interaction between components, both internally or remotely, e.g., application call stack.

---

[1] https://www.dynatrace.com
[2] https://newrelic.com
[3] https://www.appdynamics.com
[4] https://www.ca.com/us/products/ca-application-performance-management.html
[5] http://www.kieker-monitoring.net
[6] http://www.inspectit.rocks

The third activity involves presenting the collected data. The monitoring data is usually large since it is collected from many components over a long period of time. Presenting all the data to users or system operators is overwhelming and, thus, not suitable for viewing or diagnosis. The APM tools generally present the data in selected aspects to allow easier understanding by using, for example, component diagrams, sequence diagrams, and time series plots.

In the last activity, the data that is collected, stored, and presented can be interpreted and used for various purposes. Examples are problem detection and alerting, problem diagnosis and root cause isolation, and system refactoring and adaptation [HHMO17]. Problem detection and alerting employs techniques, such as statistical testings, to detect symptoms that can manifest into a failure. When such problems are detected, an alert can be triggered and system operators can be notified. Problem diagnosis and root cause isolation aim at locating the component which is responsible for the detected problem. System refactoring and adaptation try to prevent or minimize the problem by changing the configuration, e.g., scaling up the system.

2.3.5. SLAstic and Kieker

The HORA approach proposed in this thesis makes failure predictions for components based on the monitoring data collected at runtime by an APM tool. The prediction results are combined with the architectural knowledge of the system to further predict their propagations. This section introduces the SLAstic approach which provides both the monitoring data and the architectural knowledge for HORA. In Section 6.4.3, the detailed description and the extension to SLAstic will be introduced so that additional information regarding the architecture can be obtained.

SLAstic is an approach to model-driven online capacity management for component-based software systems [Hoo14]. The approach is divided into three main parts, as depicted in Figure 2.8, which are SLAstic.Monitoring, SLAstic.Reconfiguration, and SLAstic.Control. SLAstic provides frameworks and models to support online capacity management. Among others, two

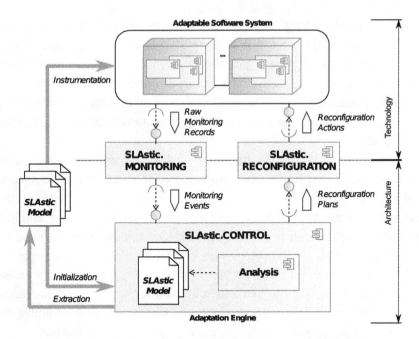

Figure 2.8.: SLAstic framework architecture [Hoo14]

components, which are the SLAstic model and the Kieker framework, provide the functionalities that are required by HORA. The SLAstic model is an architectural meta-model that is used at runtime to represent the system while the Kieker framework provides APM capability. This section introduces these two components of SLAstic. Section 2.3.5.1 describes the SLAstic model and Section 2.3.5.2 describes the Kieker framework.

2.3.5.1. SLAstic Model

SLAstic model is a runtime model that represents different aspects of component-based software systems, such as component types, deployment, reconfiguration, and usage [Hoo14]. The model provides information for system adaptation to serve the goal of model-driven online capacity management in the SLAstic framework. It contains both structural and behavioral information of a component-based software system's architecture, which is used by HORA to create a failure propagation model (Chapter 7). In a SLAstic model, the system structure is represented by four sub-models.

- *Type repository* model specifies a set of component types, including their specifications, which are used to build a system or a composite component.

- *Component assembly* model contains assembly components which are instances of component types in the type repository model.

- *Execution environment* model specifies the available execution container and their specifications, e.g., network links.

- *Component deployment* model specifies the deployment of assembly components on the execution containers.

The system behavior is represented by three sub-models.

- *Monitoring events* model contains information regarding operation execution, e.g., start and end time, and resource usage, e.g., CPU and memory utilization.

- *Trace* model contains sequences of related operation executions.

- *Usage* model contains information regarding internal and remote calls, e.g., how often one operation calls another.

The information contained in these sub-models is important to HORA since it provides insights into the system, e.g., how components are connected, deployed, and how they interact with each other. Chapter 6 introduces HORA's Architectural Dependency Model (ADM), which is an architectural model that represents dependencies between components, and how it can be extracted from a SLAstic model.

2.3.5.2. Kieker Framework

Kieker is an open-source APM framework that supports dynamic and adaptive monitoring of software systems and provides both offline and online

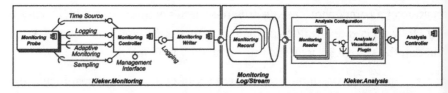

Figure 2.9.: Core components and workflow of Kieker [Hoo14]

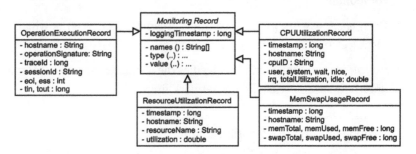

Figure 2.10.: Class diagram of monitoring records [Hoo14]

analysis of the system behavior [HWH12]. The data collection is done by instrumenting the application with monitoring probes. These probes are available in multiple programming languages and can collect various information, such as method execution time, call graph, and resource utilization. The analysis of the collected data provides insights regarding the application behavior, such as reconstructing and visualizing the architecture, and detecting anomalies.

Figure 2.9 depicts the core components and workflow of Kieker to monitor the application and analyze the monitoring data. To monitor an application, it has to be instrumented using monitoring probes that collect and write the monitoring records in a form of Kieker monitoring log or stream. The log can be stored on a file system or sent to a remote server which collects logs from distributed systems and forwards them to the analysis part. The log is then read and processed by the analysis plugins which provide various functionalities, such as trace reconstruction, architecture discovery, and anomaly detection.

Figure 2.10 illustrates the class diagram of selected Kieker monitoring records. The records contain the information regarding the executed method, e.g., the fully qualified name, when it is executed, when it finishes, and other parameters that indicate where this method is located in the call stack. The `OperationExecutionRecord`, which contains information for trace reconstruction, inherits from `MonitoringRecord` and contains the following fields:

- hostname—hostname of the machine
- operationSignature—fully qualified name of the executed method
- traceID—a unique ID of the thread that executes this method
- sessionID—a unique ID of the session
- EOI—Execution Order Index
- ESS—Execution Stack Size
- tin—the time that the method is executed
- tout—the time that the method finishes

The Execution Order Index (EOI) and Execution Stack Size (ESS) are crucial parameters that are used by SLAstic to reconstruct the trace and the call graph. EOI is the order that a method is executed. It increments for every internal or remote call to another method. ESS is the current size of the call stack. It increases when a method is called and decreases when the method finishes. Figure 2.11 illustrates an example of a trace with EOI and ESS.

HORA employs Kieker to monitor the method response time and resource utilization of an application. The component failure predictors read this information and make predictions whether the components are going to fail in the near future. The component failure predictors are presented in Chapter 5.

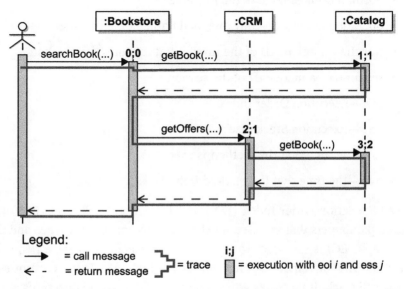

Figure 2.11.: Example of tracing with EOI and ESS [Hoo14]

3

RELATED WORK

The online failure prediction approach proposed in this thesis employs architectural knowledge of the system and failure prediction techniques. The related work involves the relevant areas in online failure prediction and architecture-based performance/reliability prediction.

The categorization of related work is based on two dimensions; 1) monolithic vs. architecture-based, and 2) offline vs. online. As outlined in Chapter 2, online prediction approaches aim at providing information regarding the near future state of the running system based on runtime observations [SLM10]. As opposed to that, offline prediction approaches are not used to trigger runtime actions, but focus on providing QoS measures to reason on system design and evolution decisions [CDI11; Mus98].

In another dimension, monolithic prediction approaches consider the system as a black box. A prediction model can be created using different techniques, such as time series forecasting or machine learning. On the other hand, architecture-based prediction approaches consider the architecture of software systems including the components and their inter-dependencies. Each component has its own specification that can be combined with the others' to form a model that represents the whole system. The relevant measures of the system can then be obtained by solving the combined model.

The related work of this thesis can be classified into four categories, based on the two dimensions, which are monolithic offline prediction, monolithic online prediction (Section 3.1), architecture-based offline prediction (Section 3.2), and architecture-based online prediction (Section 3.3). Due to the lack of relevance to our approach, we do not discuss work on monolithic offline prediction.

3.1. Monolithic Online Prediction

The HORA approach introduced in this thesis predicts online failures by combining component failure prediction with component dependencies present in the architectural knowledge. As a foundation, HORA still relies on accurate online predictions of component failures in order to further predict their consequences on other parts of the system. This section presents the related work that has been used to predict component failures in various systems.

The related work in this category has largely been collected and presented in "A survey of online failure prediction methods" by Salfner, Lenk, and Malek [SLM10]. The survey classifies related work into four main categories; failure tracking, symptom monitoring, detected error reporting, and undetected error auditing. In order not to duplicate the work, we use the same classification as presented in the survey. However, in this section, we focus on the work that has been published after the survey was carried out including those that were published prior to the survey but are highly relevant to the main contribution of this thesis. Since there is no recent work in failure tracking and undetected error auditing, these categories are not presented here. Section 3.1.1 presents the techniques that have been used to predict online failures based on symptom monitoring. Section 3.1.2 presents the prediction techniques that are based on detected error reporting.

3.1.1. Symptom Monitoring

Symptoms are the side effects that can be observed from an erroneous state of a component or system. For example, a software component that has a memory leak can cause the system to fail due to memory exhaustion. The symptom, in this case, would be the monotonic increase of the memory utilization over time. The work in this sub-category takes the symptoms as input and analyzes whether the component or the system is experiencing a failure. This section lists different techniques that have been used to predict failures by monitoring the symptoms. The techniques include function approximation (Section 3.1.1.1), classifiers (Section 3.1.1.2), system models (Section 3.1.1.3), and time series analysis (Section 3.1.1.4).

3.1.1.1. Function Approximation

Function approximation techniques use mathematical functions to relate the symptoms and the failures. The functions are created during the training phase and used at runtime to predict failures based on the symptoms.

Alonso et al. [ATBG10], Alonso, Torres, and Gavalda [ATG09], El-Shishiny, Deraz, and Badreddin [EDB08a], El-Shishiny, Deraz, and Bahy [EDB08b], Guo et al. [GJW+10], and Xue et al. [XSJC09] try to predict failures that are caused by software aging [GVVT98]. Alonso et al. [ATBG10] and Alonso, Torres, and Gavalda [ATG09] focus on software memory leakage and predict whether and when the leakage will lead to memory exhaustion. The techniques used to make prediction are linear regression and decision trees (REPtree and M5P). Instead of observing only memory usage, El-Shishiny, Deraz, and Badreddin [EDB08a] and El-Shishiny, Deraz, and Bahy [EDB08b] include performance metrics such as reponse time, and swap space, and use artificial neural networks to predict the aging. Similarly, Guo et al. [GJW+10] include the system load and use a regression model to predict the damage. Xue et al. [XSJC09] suggest that the resource exhaustion might be influenced by the workload. Thus, they include the workload into the prediction model, which is artificial neural networks.

Eckart et al. [ECHS08] predict failures in storage systems based on S.M.A.R.T. data [OP95] using Markov models. Each state in the model represents the corresponding state of the hard drives, i.e., healthy, non-healthy, and failed. The model is further extended to capture the characteristics of hard drives with RAID technology. Zhu et al. [ZWL+13] use S.M.A.R.T. data to predict drive failures by employing a backpropagation neural network model. A SVM-based method is also proposed which considers not only the raw S.M.A.R.T. data but also the rate of changes of attributes.

Baldoni et al. [BLM+12] and Baldoni, Montanari, and Rizzuto [BMR15] introduce CASPER which is a prediction framework for distributed systems. The input data is collected by sniffing network packets without the knowledge of the system or causing extra workload to the system. Complex event processing (CEP) is used to pre-process the data such as round trip time, message rate. The aggregated data is used as input for Hidden Markov model (HMM), in which two states represent a safe and unsafe states, respectively, for each kind of fault.

Leitner et al. [LMRD10; LWR+10] propose the PREvent framework which monitors system events (method or service invocation), predicts Service Level Agreement (SLA) violations, and prevents them from occurring. Multilayer perceptron is triggered to make prediction when a checkpoint will be crossed.

3.1.1.2. Classifiers

The techniques in this category classify the observed symptoms into a finite number of states, e.g., healthy or failure. The data from these states are then collected and used to create models that represent those states. At runtime, the symptoms are classified into states according to the created models and the one with the highest probability is chosen.

Al-Fuqaha et al. [ARK+10] propose a technique, called JCAA, to predict failures in telecommunication networks. The technique employs k-means to create clusters of network performance data and associate these groups with the failures. The runtime observations are classified based on these groups.

Gu et al. [GPYC08] and Gu and Wang [GW09] analyze performance metrics such as resource usage, page-in/page-out rates and use a decision tree classifier to predict failures.

Guan, Zhang, and Fu [GZF12] employ Bayesian submodels and decision trees to predict failures in computer clusters based on performance metrics. The Bayesian submodels take unlabeled data as input and classify if a data instance is an anomaly. The trees are then constructed and trained with labeled data from the Bayesian submodels.

Svendsen [Sve11] predicts failures in Unix systems by using Naïve Bayes Classifier (NBC). The input data is collected from the system such as CPU, memory, swap utilization, and I/O wait.

Magalhaes and Silva [MS10] predict performance anomalies in web applications by observing resource utilization and using machine learning algorithms, which are naïve Bayes, J48, logistic model trees, and multilayer perceptron, to create the prediction models.

Lu et al. [LWZG09] employ supervised Hessian locally linear embedding (SHLLE) algorithm to extract features from performance metrics, e.g., network traffic, resource usage, file transfer rate, and classify whether the system is deemed to fail.

Ganguly et al. [GCK+16] employ a two-step approach to predict failures in hard drives. The first step is a decision tree which classifies the drives based on the workload and SMART data. The second step is logistic regression which makes predictions for the drives in the low separation nodes of the decision tree.

3.1.1.3. System Models

System models are the models that represent the system in a normal state. The techniques in this category are based on semi-supervised learning which requires data collected during the normal state to be labeled. Models are then created based on these data. At runtime, the deviations of the symptoms from the models are regarded as anomalies or signs of pending failures.

Abed et al. [AAKR13] propose an approach to predict failures in network systems based on anomaly detection. The time series data of network parameters is split into segments and the minimum, maximum of the data in each segment is calculated and the failures are predicted using anomaly trend.

Guan, Zhang, and Fu [GZF11a; GZF11b; GZF12] collect performance metrics from computer clusters and use PCA for mutual information analysis and redundancy reduction. Bayesian submodels are employed as prediction models to classify if a data instance is anomalous.

Wang et al. [WMCT14] present a method to predict failures in hard drives. The method is composed of two steps. First, the S.M.A.R.T. data is aggregated and transformed by Mahalanobis distance and Box-Cox into one index. Second, the Generalized Likelihood Ratio Test (GLRT) is used to detect the number of anomalies in each window. If the threshold is violated, a warning is issued.

3.1.1.4. Time Series Analysis

The techniques in this category take time series data as input and extrapolate it to predict the value in the future. The failures can be predicted from the future value by using a threshold. For example, if the memory utilization is predicted to cross the threshold defined by the amount of available memory, then a failure can be expected. The techniques in this category are also used by HORA to predict failures based on time series data (Section 5.4).

Cavallo, Di Penta, and Canfora [CDC10] compare different time series forecasting techniques to predict response time violations of web services. The results are used to support QoS-aware service selection.

Cui et al. [CLL+12] investigate the difference of software aging in physical and virtual environments and propose a way to detect and predict the aging. Linear regression is used to detect the trend and predict the resource exhaustion time which implies a failure.

Amin, Colman, and Grunske [ACG11; ACG12] predict the QoS of web services based on the response time by using time series analysis. Amin, Colman, and Grunske [ACG11] employ a statistical approach, named CREQA, to detect changes in the response time which may lead to failures. Amin, Colman, and Grunske [ACG12] integrate Autoregressive Integrated Moving Average (ARIMA) and Generalized Autoregressive Conditional Heteroskedasticity (GARCH) models to improve the prediction. The ARIMA model is first constructed from the QoS data and the forecast residual is used to constructed the GARCH model.

3.1.2. Detected Error Reporting

Errors are direct effects that can be seen from a component or system in an incorrect state. They are, for instance, error messages in the application or system logs. The techniques in this category aim to analyze the errors or their patterns that precede failures. When these patterns are recognized at runtime, it is likely that a failure will follow.

3.1.2.1. Rule-Based Approaches

The techniques in this category analyze the events in the logs and create rules of how the events occur before the failures. At runtime, the detected events are compared against the rules and the matched rule is used to predict failures.

Clemm and Hartwig [CH10] propose NETradamus which is a framework for forecasting failures from event messages. The framework mines the event messages in the log files and creates rules that represent the events. These rules are used as case bases at runtime to predict failure events.

Gu et al. [GZL+08] present a dynamic meta-learning prediction which allows the predictors to be re-trained at runtime. The re-training is done by dividing data into three parts: 1) historical data except the most recent one is used for re-training, 2) the most recent data is used for testing and rule adjustment, and 3) the prediction set which is the current data to be used for making prediction. The rules that result in low precision and recall are excluded from the next generation of the predictor.

Fu et al. [FRZ+12] propose LogMaster which is a set of algorithms that mines event correlations from log messages. Apriori-LIS, which is an extension of Apriori algorithm, is proposed and used to mine the event rules. Event correlation graphs (ECGS) is introduced to represent these rules. The ECGs are used at runtime to match events with the rules and to calculate the probability of a failure event.

Zheng et al. [ZLG+10] propose a method to predict failures with lead time and failure location in the Blue Gene supercomputer. The rules are created by analyzing log patterns that precede failures. The lead time is calculated by the time between last event until the failure occurrence. A genetic algorithm is then used to generate more rules during the training for failure prediction.

Yu et al. [YZLC11] compare two widely-used approaches, which are period-based and event-based, to predict failures in the Blue Gene/P supercomputer. A Bayesian prediction model is used to evaluate the accuracy of both methods and the results show that the event-based approach outperforms the period-based approach.

Liang et al. [LZXS07b] split log files into windows and extract the statistics of events into features. Different machine learning algorithms are applied to learn the extracted features and predict whether a failure is pending.

3.1.2.2. Pattern Recognition

Pattern recognition analyzes the data and identifies the patterns between errors and failures. In contrast to rule-based approaches, pattern recognition employs complex models, e.g., machine learning, to represent these relationships. The HORA approach also employs techniques in this category to predict failures based on event log (Section 5.5) and S.M.A.R.T. data (Section 5.6).

Fulp, Fink, and Haack [FFH08] employ SVM to predict failures from log files. A sliding window is used to extract sub-sequences of log messages. The extracted sequences are transformed to a frequency representation and used as input to the SVM. The SVM then associates these sequences to classes which represents failure and non-failure states of the system.

Gainaru et al. [GCF+11] propose an event prediction approach for High Performance Computing (HPC) which uses an adaptive time window. The log files are preprocessed by counting the number of occurrences of each log pattern. These numbers are used to build memory Markov chains which represent the probability of an event occurring after the others. At runtime, if the the prediction quality drops, the model is updated by monitoring the pattern distribution and recalculate their confidence values.

Fullop, Gainaru, and Plutchak [FGP12] propose an approach to predict events based on log files. The event correlations are extracted from the pre-processed logs and used to create a directed graph to represent inter-relationships between events. This graph is used as a reference to detect patterns of events at runtime which may precede certain events.

Fronza et al. [FSS+12] employ random indexing which assigns an index vector to each event in the logs of software applications. Based on these index vectors, context vectors are calculated and used as input for SVM. The SVM is weighted to cope with skewed classes and is used with linear, polynomial and radial basis kernels.

Watanabe et al. [WOS+12] propose an approach for real-time learning failure prediction based on log files. The log files are collected from cloud servers with several virtual machines. The similarity between each log record is computed based on the words contained in the log message. Each record is assigned a unique ID and the sequence of IDs is used to form an error sequence. The Bayesian method is used to calculate the probability of a failure that follows the sequence. The evaluation is done compared to NBC which uses individual log records to calculate the probability model.

Ge [Ge11] proposes a failure prediction framework that predicts failures in supercomputers. The event logs of Blue Gene/L are first categorized into clusters where each cluster represents the same pattern of messages. Based on these clusters, the semi-Markov CRF models are constructed and used to predict the failures.

Theera-Ampornpunt, Zhou, and Bagchi [TZB11] present an approach to improve the prediction of time to failure. The approach uses a set of HMMs, where each one is trained with different lead times, e.g., 40 seconds or

80 seconds. At runtime, the HMM that matches the current input sequence with the highest probability is used to make predictions.

Sonoda, Watanabe, and Matsumoto [SWM12] predict the time of failure occurrence based on system logs using message pattern learning. The messages are first classified into groups by using a similarity check. Bayesian learning then calculates the probability of the failures occurring after the message patterns. The lead times of the failures are computed by averaging the time-to-failure of the same message pattern in the training data.

Shalan and Zulkernine [SZ13] present an approach for failure mode prediction. The error log records are analyzed to create error signatures which summarize error log variables for each failure mode. A predictive function is created for each mode based on these signatures and used to predict failures at runtime.

Nakka, Agrawal, and Choudhary [NAC11] employs data mining to predict failures in HPC. The usage data and failure logs are collected from supercomputing clusters. The information, such as idle time and time since last failure, is extracted from the data and used to train decision tree-based predictors. At runtime, the predictors classify the data and make predictions if a failure would occur in one hour.

Kimura et al. [KWTI15] propose an approach to learn the log message patterns and predict failures in large-scale networks. The logs are categorized into groups that have the same patterns. SVM is used to learn the patterns that lead to the failures and make predictions at runtime.

3.2. Architecture-based Offline Prediction

The approaches in this category employ architecture-based system models annotated with specific quality evaluation models or scenarios [BG04; BZJ04; Gru07], e.g., with respect to performance [BDIS04; Koz10], reliability [GT01], and safety [GH08] attributes. The model can be solved by using analytical solution or simulations to obtain the relevant properties of the whole system. The concept of these approaches has been previously introduced in Section 2.3.

Cheung [Che80] proposes a seminal software reliability model that takes into account the reliability of individual components along with the probability of calling other components. A Markov model is employed to combine the reliability of components and represent the reliability of the whole system. Cortellessa and Grassi [CG07] present an approach for reliability analysis of component-based software systems. Based on the system architecture, they consider the error propagation probability between components in addition to the reliability of individual components. Becker, Koziolek, and Reussner [BKR09] introduce the Palladio Component Model (PCM) which enables performance prediction of component-based software systems. Brosch [Bro12] extends the PCM by annotating the components with corresponding reliability attributes. The model is transformed into a discrete-time Markov chain and solved to obtain the reliability of the system. Uhle and Tröger [UT14] employ dependency graphs to assess dependability of microservice applications. The graphs are used to construct qualitative and quantitative fault trees for the corresponding applications.

3.3. Architecture-based Online Prediction

As a recent example for performance, Huber et al. [HBS+17] employ an architecture-based performance model to predict system performance at runtime for capacity planning and online resource provisioning. The performance characteristics are captured in an architectural performance model which is then solved by transforming it to an analytical model or by simulation, similar to Becker, Koziolek, and Reussner [BKR09]. Although this work can be applied to predict performance-related failures, i.e., timing failures [ALRL04], it does not consider content failures. Hora takes a different approach by predicting both timing and content failures that result from the failure of each component which propagates through the architecture until it reaches the system boundary.

Chalermarrewong, Achalakul, and See [CAS12] predict system unavailability in data centers using a set of component predictors and fault tree analysis. The component predictors employ ARMA to predict failures of hardware components. These component failures are leaf nodes in the fault tree which is evaluated to conclude whether the current set of component failures will lead to system unavailability. Even though this work does not consider software, it shares the same basic idea as HORA by having a dedicated failure predictor for each component. However, the fault tree does not incorporate the conditional probability which represents complex software architectural relationships. On the other hand, HORA employs Bayesian network theory which can represent conditional dependencies and infer the probabilities of failures and their propagation.

Capelastegui et al. [CNH+13] present an online failure prediction system for private IaaS platforms. The system takes as input both data from the virtual and physical machines. The data, which is resource usage, application logs, and failure data, is sent to a monitoring and prediction server. Three different prediction mechanisms are used to predict failures based on the three data types, namely, resource exhaustion, event-based, and failure-based. The proposed prediction approach is tightly coupled with the cloud infrastructure, i.e., only the vertical composition of physical and virtual machines are considered in the failure propagation. In contrast, HORA considers both horizontal and vertical compositions, i.e., the failure propagation between software components and the propagation between software and hardware components. Furthermore, the proposed approach does not consider probabilistic failure propagation while HORA explicitly considers the propagation probabilities in the Failure Propagation Model (Chapter 7).

Mohamed [Moh12] proposes an approach to predict software functional failures at runtime based on error spread-signature. The error spread-signature is obtained by instrumenting the program to output the information regarding the control flow. A connection dependency graph (CDG) is introduced to represent this information. However, the CDG does not consider the probabilistic propagation of the failures between components. On the contrary, HORA aims to predict QoS-related failures and also includes the failure propagation probabilities in the prediction model.

Pertet and Narasimhan [PN05b] propose a topology-aware approach to detect and handle cascading failures in computer networks. The idea is that each node in the network has some knowledge about the topology, e.g., what is the next node it connects to. The system then uses this information to traverse the network and identify the problematic node. This approach focuses on predicting cascading failures of nodes in computer networks and does not consider how a failure propagates inside a node. In contrast, HORA aims to predict failures in software systems by considering how a failure of one component or sub-component can propagate to the others through the architectural dependencies.

Part II.

Contribution

4

Research Design and

Overview of the Approach

This chapter presents the research design of the thesis and the overview of the approach. Section 4.1 describes the goal and the research questions. Section 4.2 presents the research plan. Section 4.3 describes the overview of the proposed prediction approach.

4.1. Goal and Research Questions

This section describes the goal of this thesis and the research questions which will be addressed. These questions will be further divided into subquestions and described in detail.

The goal of this thesis is to *improve prediction quality of online failure prediction in software systems.*

When a component in a system fails, the failure affects not only that component but also other components in the system. We hypothesize that the components that are affected by this failure may be determined by the

Research question		Investigated in
RQ1:	How can the failures of individual components in the system be accurately predicted?	
RQ1.1:	Which component measures are available and can be used to predict failures at runtime?	Chapter 5
RQ1.2:	Which prediction techniques should be applied to which types of measures?	Chapter 5
RQ1.3:	What are the prediction qualities of component failure predictors?	Chapters 10 to 12
RQ2:	How can architectural information be used to improve online failure prediction?	
RQ2.1:	Which architectural information can be used to improve online failure prediction?	Chapter 6
RQ2.2:	How can the required architectural information for online failure prediction be modeled?	Chapter 6
RQ2.3:	Does architectural information affect the prediction quality? If yes, to which extent?	Chapter 13
RQ3:	How can component failure prediction and architectural information be combined to improve online failure prediction?	
RQ3.1:	What is a suitable model to represent the combined information?	Chapter 7
RQ3.2:	What is the prediction quality of the combined model?	Chapter 13
RQ3.3:	What is the scalability of the combined model?	Chapter 13

Table 4.1.: Research questions

architectural dependency graph which describes how components depend on each other. If the component failures can be accurately predicted and the dependencies between components are known, it should be possible to predict the propagation of the failures. This would allow to determine if a failure would cause the system to fail, either partially or entirely.

In order to achieve this goal, we propose an online failure prediction approach, called HORA. HORA employs online failure prediction techniques to predict failures of individual components and combines the prediction results with architectural knowledge. The combined model can infer new probabilities of component failures taking into account the failures of other components in the system.

In this section, three research questions are raised and described. Table 4.1 lists the questions, the subquestions, and the corresponding chapters in which the questions are investigated and answered. The questions are detailed in the remainder of this section.

RQ1: How can the failures of individual components in the system be accurately predicted?

Predicting failures of each component in the system is the first step to predicting the effects of the failures on the whole system. There already exists a large body of work for online failure prediction. However, a system is usually composed of different types of components, i.e., hardware and software components. Each component produces different types of data that can be used as input for the prediction method.

This research question, which is split into three subquestions, aims to answer which prediction techniques are suitable for which types of components.

RQ1.1: Which component measures are available and can be used to predict failures at runtime?

Predicting component failures requires the information that can represent the status of each component. Different measures are available depending on the type of the components. For instance, hardware components, e.g., CPU, memory, and hard drives, have measures related to the utilization level. On the other hand, software components, e.g., class methods, databases, external services, would produce response time as measures. This research question will investigate which measures can be obtained from which types of components and which ones can represent the status and can be used to predict component failures.

RQ1.2: Which prediction techniques should be applied to which types of measures?

Different types of measures can be obtained from different types of components. However, not all failure prediction techniques can be applied to all types of available measures. For example, time series forecasting techniques are obviously suitable for time series data. If the data is event-based, other techniques have to be employed. This question will investigate which prediction techniques are suitable for predicting component failures based on different types of data.

RQ1.3: What are the prediction qualities of component failure predictors?

The prediction quality of each individual component failure predictor is the foundation of the HORA approach. In order to make an accurate prediction for the whole system, the failure prediction of each component has to be accurate. This question will investigate how accurate the component failure predictors are.

RQ2: How can architectural information be used to improve online failure prediction?

Architectural dependency plays an important role in the propagation of the failures. A failing component can cause other components to fail if there are dependencies between them. For example, in a three-tier architecture, a failing database can cause the business tier to fail because the transaction may not be completed. However, this failure is not caused by the business tier itself but it originates from the database and propagates through the dependency chain. Thus, predicting this type of failure may not be accomplished only by monitoring each component separately. Furthermore, although predicting the failure of the database can be achieved, predicting its effects on other components is not trivial.

This research question is divided into three following subquestions.

RQ2.1: Which architectural information can be used to improve online failure prediction?

Architectural information of the system, e.g., a dependency graph, gives information regarding the dependencies between components. However, the granularity of this information plays an important role. For example, a high-level dependency graph may not contain sufficient information regarding how failures propagate. On the other hand, a fine-grained dependency graph may contain much more information than needed, which can complicate the analysis. This research question will investigate which information and how much details are required in order to improve the prediction of cascading failures.

RQ2.2: How can the required architectural information for online failure prediction be modeled?

In order to achieve the prediction of failure propagation, a suitable representation is needed to capture the architectural dependency information of components in the system. There exists already a number of architectural models which represent different aspects of software system, such as performance or reliability models (Section 2.3). This research question aims to investigate whether the existing models are suitable for representing architectural dependency information. If not, then a new model will be introduced and investigated.

RQ2.3: Does architectural information affect the prediction quality? If yes, to which extent?

The architectural dependency model can be created in different ways, either manually or automatically. For manual creation, the model can be created by system experts who have detailed knowledge about the system structure and behavior. Automatic extraction can be done by gathering information from other architectural models. The extraction algorithm also plays a role in the final model. The resulting models from these methods can be different and may produce different prediction results. This research question aims to investigate if different granularity of the architectural dependency models will affect the prediction quality.

RQ3: How can component failure prediction and architectural information be combined to improve online failure prediction?

The component failure prediction provides predictions of when a component in the system will fail. The architectural dependency information provides the information of how components in the system depend on each other. In order to predict system failure, these two pieces of information have to be combined.

This research question is divided into the three following subquestions.

RQ3.1: What is a suitable model to represent the combined information?

The architectural dependency model obtained in RQ2 contains the required information about the dependencies. However, since it represents only the dependencies between component pairs, it may not be suitable for inferring failure probabilities through the dependency chain of the whole system. This question will investigate the suitability of the architectural dependency model for online failure prediction. If it is not suitable, then a new model will be introduced and investigated.

RQ3.2: What is the prediction quality of the combined model?

At runtime, the prediction model, which is created by combining the architectural dependency information and the component failure prediction, needs to be solved to obtain the probability of cascading failures. This question aims to investigate the prediction quality of the combined model.

RQ3.3: What is the scalability of the combined model?

The model that is used to predict cascading failures needs to incorporate the architectural information of the system. For a large distributed system, the number of components can be very high. Furthermore, the prediction needs to be carried out in realtime which includes analyzing monitoring data of all components and inferring failure probability from the model. This question aims to investigate the scalability of the model when applied to predict failures in large distributed systems.

4.2. Research Plan

In order to answer the research questions and to achieve the defined goal, the research plan of this thesis is split into four work packages.

4.2.1. WP1: Component failure prediction

This work package aims to investigate the prediction of individual component failures independently from each other. Different types of monitoring data from different components will be collected. The data will then be investigated to see which prediction techniques are suitable for them. The existing prediction techniques will also be investigated to see if they provide sufficient information regarding component failures, i.e., the expected time and probability of the pending failures. If the existing prediction techniques cannot provide the required information, an investigation will be carried out to determine what would be the required extensions. This work package addresses the research questions RQ1.1 and RQ1.2.

4.2.2. WP2: Architectural dependency modeling

This work package comprises the construction of the architectural dependency model that will provide propagation information. This information will be used to predict cascading failures. An investigation will be carried out to see which architectural information can represent the propagation of the failures. The existing architectural models (Section 2.3) will be investigated to see if they contain the required architectural information. If this information is not in the models, further studies will be carried out to see if they can be obtained from the available sources of information, e.g., application traces, and if they can be included into the models. This work package addresses the research questions RQ2.1 and RQ2.2.

4.2.3. WP3: Failure propagation prediction

This work package aims at combining the component failure prediction techniques (WP1) with the architectural dependency model (WP2). The architectural dependency model provides the information regarding component dependencies and how failures can propagate through the system architecture. The component failure prediction techniques provide the probabilities of components failing in the near future. The result is a combined model that can predict both the failure of individual components and their propagation. In this work package, different techniques will be investigated to see which one is most suitable to represent the combined information. This work package addresses the research question RQ3.1.

4.2.4. WP4: Evaluation

This work package aims to evaluate each part of the proposed approach. The first part will focus on evaluating the prediction quality of the component failure predictors. For this part, a quantitative evaluation will be carried out. Different prediction techniques will be applied to different types of data. The second part focuses on a quantitative evaluation of the failure propagation model which combines both the component failure predictors and the architectural dependency model. This part will evaluate the prediction quality of the failure propagation model, the effect of the architectural dependency model on the prediction, and the scalability of the failure propagation model. This work package addresses the research questions RQ1.3, RQ2.3, RQ3.2, and RQ3.3.

4.3. Overview of the HORA Approach

The HORA approach aims to improve online failure prediction by combining online failure prediction techniques with the architectural knowledge to predict if and when a failure of a component will propagate to other components and affect other parts of the system. Figure 4.1 depicts the architecture of the HORA approach. The approach can be divided into three main steps. The first step, denoted by ①, is component failure prediction which focuses on predicting the failure of each individual component. The second step, denoted by ②, is architectural dependency modeling which aims to represent the dependencies between components in the system. The third step, denoted by ③, is failure propagation modeling which combines the results of component failure prediction from ① and the architectural dependency model from ②. The resulting model can infer the probability

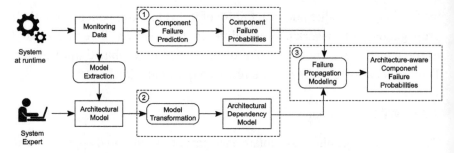

Figure 4.1.: High-level overview of the HORA approach

of component failures taking into account the propagation paths based on the architectural dependencies.

The overall vision of the HORA approach presented here has been published in a short paper [PHG14]. The details of the approach, which includes all three steps, an implementation of HORA, and an extensive evaluation have been presented in a journal paper [POHG18]. The component failure predictors have been presented in three papers [PGK+14; PHG13; POHG16].

4.3.1. Component Failure Prediction

Predicting when a component will encounter a problem at runtime is the first step to predicting a failure of the whole system. A system is usually composed of a large number of different types of components, i.e., hardware and software, which serve different purposes. Each of them produces different types of symptoms and errors which can reflect its health status. Selecting the relevant data and the suitable prediction technique for each component is a non-trivial task. Furthermore, each predictor needs to be optimized for failure prediction of that component. Three different types of monitoring data considered in this thesis are:

- Time series data that is collected from hardware resource utilization, e.g., CPU utilization, and software components, e.g., method and service response times.

- Event logs which are collected from High Performance Computing (HPC) infrastructure

- Self-Monitoring, Analysis and Reporting Technology (S.M.A.R.T.) data which is collected from hard drives

For each type of data, suitable prediction techniques are selected and used to create prediction models. The models are then used to predict failures of each component.

Chapter 5 provides the concepts and details of component failure prediction based on these three types of monitoring data.

4.3.2. Architectural Dependency Modeling

The second part focuses on creating a model (ADM) that can represent the dependencies between components. The model will be used to deduce to which extent a failure of one component will affect another. For example, in *Running Example 1* (Figure 1.1), business-tier instances (BT) that make remote calls to update the database would be more likely to fail if the database fails since there is a direct dependency. In contrast, if they do not make remote calls to the database, they would not be affected by the database failure because they are not dependent.

The model can be created manually or automatically either by static or dynamic analysis. However, in this thesis, automated dynamic analysis is employed since it can extract the actual runtime behavior of the system, e.g., control flow, number of calls between components, and deployment information. This information is the key to compute how much a component depends on another. For instance, the more the business-tier instances make remote calls to the database, the more likely the business-tier instances would experience a problem if the database has failed. The model acts as an intermediate step between different types of architectural models and the final model (Failure Propagation Model (FPM)) which is used to infer the failure propagation. The ADM that contains only the information required for the online failure prediction allows the next step, which is failure propagation modeling, to be decoupled from the architectural models. It also allows the ADM to be transformed from different architectural models that already exist.

Chapter 6 describes the concept of architectural dependency modeling in detail, including how it can be extracted from the runtime monitoring data collected by dynamic analysis.

4.3.3. Failure Propagation Modeling

Failure propagation modeling focuses on creating a model that can combine the results of the first two parts to predict the failure of the whole system. The prediction results obtained from component failure predictors are used as a basis that indicate the failures caused by the components themselves—without effects from the others. The architectural model in the second step is transformed into another representation (FPM) so that it is more suitable for inferring the effects of failures across the whole architecture of the system. At regular intervals, the component failure probabilities are fed into the FPM and the model is solved to obtain the added failure probabilities propagated from other components in the dependency chain. With this method, the failure probability of the whole system, i.e., the service at the system boundary, can then be inferred.

Chapter 7 provides the details of the FPM, how it can be obtained, and how the inference is carried out.

4.3.4. Implementation

In this thesis, we provide two implementations of the HORA approach. The first implementation aims at assessing whether combining component failure prediction and architectural knowledge can improve online failure prediction. This implementation allows the evaluation to be repeated multiple times using different datasets to obtain statistically significant results.

The second implementation aims at providing HORA as a tool that can be used to predict failures in production systems at runtime. It provides interfaces to services that are available at runtime which are storage for monitoring data, prediction algorithms, and visualization of prediction results.

COMPONENT FAILURE
PREDICTION

The first step in predicting system failures is to predict failures of individual components. Different types of components generate different types of data that can reflect the health of the components. Thus, suitable techniques have to be selected and optimized to predict component failures with high prediction quality. This chapter presents three categories of techniques that are adapted and extended to predict failures of different types of components.

Section 5.1 presents the research questions that will be answered in this chapter. Section 5.2 presents the overview of the component failure prediction. Section 5.3 details the requirements for the component failure predictors. Section 5.4 presents an approach to predict failures based on time series data. Section 5.5 presents how event logs can be used to predict critical events. Section 5.6 presents an approach for hard drive failure prediction. Section 5.7 summarizes the contribution of this chapter. In addition to these three techniques, the existing techniques listed in Section 3.1 can also be applied to predict component failures.

5.1. Research Questions

This chapter aims to answer the following research questions which have been previously stated in detail in Section 4.1:

- RQ1.1: Which component measures are available and can be used to predict failures at runtime?

- RQ1.2: Which prediction techniques should be applied to which types of measures?

5.2. Overview of Component Failure Prediction

Figure 5.1 depicts the overview of component failure prediction of HORA. In the first step, the monitoring data is collected and separated for individual components in the system. For each component, there is one dedicated failure predictor, which is responsible for predicting the failures of that specific component. Then, the prediction is executed regularly at runtime,

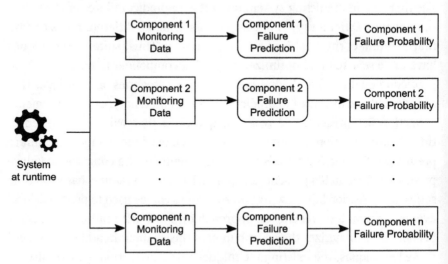

Figure 5.1.: Overview of component failure prediction

based on a pre-defined lead time, to provide the most up-to-date information regarding the component status. The output of the prediction, which is a component failure probability, indicates the likelihood of a component failure based on the given lead time. Lastly, this information is passed on to the Failure Propagation Model (FPM), which will be described in Chapter 7.

5.3. Requirements of Component Failure Predictors

The HORA approach to online failure prediction is designed to be modular and extensible which means it does not enforce specific techniques to be used as component failure predictors. Different prediction techniques can be used for different types of components if they are suitable and produce good results. However, they have to conform to the following input and output interfaces:

- Input

    - *Monitoring data.* The most recent monitoring data of a component is provided to the prediction algorithm. This ensures that the prediction is made based on the latest information regarding the status of the component. However, the amount of data depends on the application. A small amount of data may not sufficiently represent the true behavior and results in an inaccurate prediction. On the other hand, a large amount of data may include past behavior that is outdated and no longer represents the current status of the component.

    - *Lead time.* The lead time indicates how far into the future should the forecast be made. The further into the future the forecast is, the less accurate it is. Nonetheless, a forecast in the very near future may not provide enough time for the system administrators to prepare for the upcoming failures.

- Output

  – *Component failure probability.* The component failure probability indicates how likely a component is going to fail at the time indicated by the lead time. This probability is based on the monitoring data collected from one component and does not consider the failures of other components and the architectural knowledge.

5.4. Time Series-based Failure Prediction

Time series data is one of the most common types of monitoring data collected from software systems. Examples of these are service response time, method response time, CPU utilization, and memory utilization. These data can be interpreted to reflect the health of the component. For instance, an increasing response time of the service may indicate an internal error or an increasing memory utilization over a long period may be caused by a memory leak in a software component.

Figure 5.2 illustrates the concept of a component failure predictor based on the memory consumption of a business-tier instance in *Running Example 1* (Figure 1.1). The plot shows that the memory utilization constantly increases over time until 3:35PM. This may indicate a fault which is a memory leak in the software component. If the utilization continues to increase and reaches 100%, the system may crash or start swapping. The memory swapping can cause the system to slow down and fail to respond to the requests in a timely manner. In this example, our goal is to predict the probability of the memory utilization reaching 100% at 3:55PM.

Predicting failures based on time series data is composed of three steps. First, if the data is not strictly time series data, i.e., not equally spaced in time, a preprocessing step is required to transform them into time series data. Second, a forecasting algorithm is applied to extrapolate the observed data into the future. Third, a method is needed to interpret the extrapolation and estimate the failure probability. These three steps are discussed in detail in the following subsections.

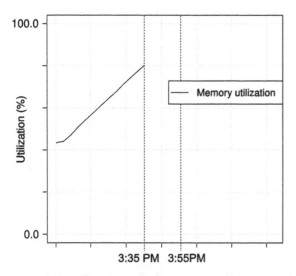

Figure 5.2.: Memory utilization of a business-tier instance of *Running Example 1*

5.4.1. Preprocessing

Time series data is usually collected at regular intervals, e.g., every 10 seconds, where the data points are equally spaced in time. This is true for some data sources, e.g., CPU or memory utilization, whose data can be directly used as input for forecasting algorithms. However, data sources that do not generate time series, e.g., service response times which are not invoked at regular intervals, will produce event-based data. In order to apply forecasting algorithms, a preprocessing step is required which transforms them into time series data.

The method used to transform data to time series is data aggregation. Data aggregation divides a sequence of data into time windows of equal length. Each window is large enough to make sure that there it contains at least one data point. For each window, an aggregation method, e.g., mean, median, or percentile, is applied to the data points in that window to compute a new value. The result of this process is time series data of which data points are equally spaced by the length of the aggregation window.

5.4.2. Time Series Forecasting

Once the data is transformed into time series, any time series forecasting algorithms can be applied to predict future values. In the current implementation, HORA employs ARIMA (Section 2.2.1) to make forecasts for the time series data obtained from the preprocessing step. However, only the most recent monitoring data is fed to the prediction algorithm so that the current behavior of the component is contained in the data. In addition to the data, the lead time is also provided to the prediction algorithm. The output of the time series forecasting is obtained as a predicted value and the prediction interval, namely the upper and the lower bounds.

5.4.3. Failure Prediction

The goal of time series forecasting is to predict the future value of the data. However, the predicted value alone is not sufficient for predicting a pending failure because there is no definition of failure in order to classify the predicted value. The method of predicting failure based on time series data of HORA is based on an assumption that the component will fail if the observed data crosses a certain threshold. This section describes how the failure thresholds are set for different types of components.

In practice, the SLO is usually defined for the service, i.e., response time of the service at system boundary. Thus, a solution is needed to set failure thresholds for the internal components. Furthermore, there are virtual resources that are obtained from the monitoring, e.g., load average, and setting the failure threshold is a non-trivial task.

In order to define proper failure thresholds, the types of data sources are divided into three following categories.

1. Service—Setting the failure threshold of a service is straightforward since the required service level is usually specified by the SLO. The threshold may be defined in two ways. First, the response time of a service at the system boundary can be specified. The requests that take longer than this pre-defined value are then classified as failures.

However, the response time can also be specified for a certain period of time, e.g., the 95th percentile of the response times of all requests in a 1-minute window must not exceed the threshold. Second, the ratio of successful Hypertext Transfer Protocol (HTTP) requests may also be specified. For example, the ratio of successful requests over all requests in a 1-minute window must be greater than or equal to 99.99%.

2. Software components and third-party services—The response times of software components may vary depending on the functions that need to be executed. Some components may take longer to execute while some may return almost immediately. Setting these thresholds manually is, however, not feasible since a system may contain a large number of internal methods. A more practical way that is implemented in HORA is to set the failure thresholds of all software components to the same value as the service. Since the response times of internal components are always smaller than or equal to that of the service, this ensures that if one of the components exceeds the threshold, the service will also exceed the threshold as well.

3. Hardware components—Similar to monitoring the response time of software components, the failure thresholds of hardware components can be specified by monitoring the metrics that can indicate the health of the components. These thresholds correspond to different measures depending on the type of the hardware. For example, the failure threshold of the memory can be specified by the utilization which is 100%. The failure threshold of the CPU can be defined based on the load average. The load average represents the number of tasks in the CPU queue over time which reflects the status of the CPU better than the CPU utilization [Wal06]. For instance, a 1-minute load average of 1.0 means that there is one task in the CPU queue on average in the past minute. If the machine is equipped with two CPUs, the failure threshold of the load average would be 2.

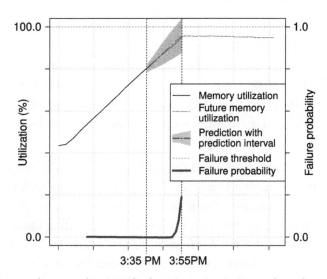

Figure 5.3.: Failure prediction of a business-tier instance based on the memory utilization

Figure 5.3 depicts how a failure prediction is carried out based on the observed memory utilization in Figure 5.2. Since the memory utilization is time series data, we can, for instance, employ ARIMA [SS11] as a component failure prediction technique. The goal of the prediction is to predict when the memory utilization will reach the 100% threshold, assuming that the machine will have a performance degradation when the memory is depleted, which can cause a service failure. The thin solid line in the graph indicates the monitoring data of memory utilization up to 3:35 PM. The dash-dotted line indicates the prediction of the memory utilization in the next 20 minutes with a prediction interval in light grey.

The probability of the monitoring data crossing the failure threshold α can be computed using the probability density function $f(x)$ of the predicted performance measure as

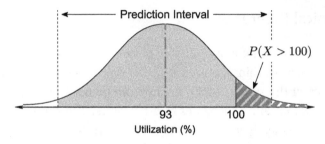

Figure 5.4.: Probability density function of memory utilization at 3:55 PM and memory failure probability

$$P(X > \alpha) = \int_{\alpha}^{\infty} f(x)dx \qquad (5.1)$$

$$= 1 - \int_{-\infty}^{\alpha} f(x)dx \qquad (5.2)$$

Figure 5.4 depicts the probability density function of the memory utilization at 3:55 PM. Assuming that the input data is normally distributed, the prediction error is also normally distributed [MRH09]. Thus, the prediction interval assembles a normal distribution and the Equation 5.2 can be written as

$$P(X > \alpha) = 1 - \frac{1}{2}\left[1 + \mathrm{erf}\left(\frac{\alpha - \mu}{\sigma\sqrt{2}}\right)\right] \qquad (5.3)$$

The mean and the standard deviation of the distribution can be computed based on the predicted value and the prediction interval. In this example, the predicted value of 93% indicates the mean of the distribution, μ. The standard deviation, σ, can be computed based on the 95% prediction interval which covers the $\pm 1.96\sigma$ area of the distribution [MRH09]. The probability of the memory utilization crossing the failure threshold at 100% can be computed by substituting μ, σ, and α in the Equation 5.3.

5.5. Critical Event Prediction

Log files are one of the most valuable piece of information. They contain execution traces, warnings, error messages, etc., which represent the status of each part of the system [OS07]. They can be used to analyze how the problem develops and propagates to other parts. The simplest way of log analysis is to manually investigate its contents. However, for large systems which produce several gigabytes of log files, this is a time-consuming task and is infeasible in practice. Furthermore, the analysis is usually done after the system has already experienced a problem to investigate the root cause and does not help prevent the problem from occurring at runtime.

This section introduces critical event prediction which aims to analyze the log messages at runtime and predict the problems that may occur in advance. The prediction employs machine learning techniques to identify and learn the patterns in the log messages that are the signs of possible problems.

The core components of the critical event prediction are *(i.)* event preprocessing, *(ii.)* event classification, and *(iii.)* event prediction. The goal of the preprocessing is to prepare the event streams for the subsequent steps. First, the events are normalized, e.g., replacing numbers and identifiers by generic template placeholders. Second, the amount of log data is reduced on-the-fly by removing redundant/similar log events observed in a configurable time window. The algorithm used for the preprocessing is based on Adaptive Semantic Filtering (ASF) [LZXS07a] and Duplicate Removal Filter (DRF) that we have developed. Both filters remove redundant messages by considering the similarity coefficient between them. The event classification and prediction are both based on machine learning techniques although they have different purposes. The event classification aims to identify the type of event based on the log messages while event prediction aims to predict whether specific types of events will occur in the future.

The overview of the prediction is depicted in Figure 5.5. The workflow is split into two phases, namely training and prediction phases. The prediction models are created during the training phase and used to predict critical events during the prediction phase. The red line denotes the critical event

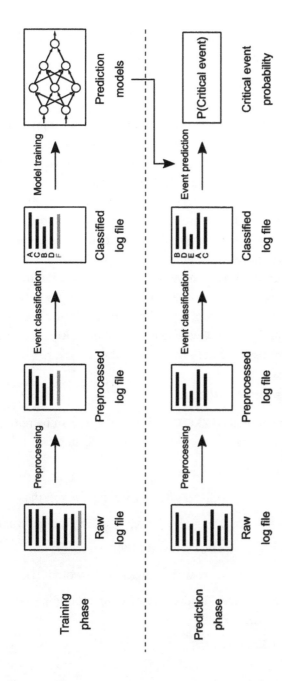

Figure 5.5.: Overview of critical event prediction

that we would like to predict. The letters A–F are example labels used to classified events into similar groups.

5.5.1. Preprocessing

Log files of large systems usually contain huge amounts of log entries. However, many of the log entries contain redundant information, as a single root cause may trigger multiple components of the system to write log entries to the file. Moreover, the components may even produce different log messages for the same root cause. Redundant log entries describe the same information and are not of interest for machine learning purposes. In order to remove redundant log events, we employ a combination of log message normalization and filtering, as detailed in Sections 5.5.1.1 and 5.5.1.2. The key idea behind the filtering is to remove redundant information by considering the time gap and the semantic correlation between two log records. For the filtering, we use the approach of Adaptive Semantic Filtering (ASF) Liang et al. [LZXS07a] and our Duplicate Removal Filter (DRF). A part from the original ASF is also used for the log normalization.

5.5.1.1. Log Message Normalization

As proposed by Liang et al. [LZXS07a], log messages can be normalized by applying transformations that include the following steps:

1. Removing punctuation, e.g., .   ; :   ?   !   = - [ ] | < > +

2. Removing definite and indefinite articles, e.g., *a, an, the*

3. Removing weak words, e.g., *be, is are, of, at, such, after, from*

4. Replacing all numbers by the word NUMBER

5. Replacing all hex addresses with *N* digits by the word NDigitHex_Addr

6. Replacing domain specific identifiers by corresponding words such as REGISTER or DIRECTORY

7. Replacing all dates by DATE

```
4 torus receiver x+ input pipe error(s) (dcr 0x02ec) detected
1 torus receiver x- input pipe error(s) (dcr 0x02ed) detected
191790399 L3 EDRAM error(s) (dcr 0x0157) detected
2 L3 EDRAM error(s) (dcr 0x0157) detected
Error receiving packet, expecting type 57
3 torus receiver y+ input pipe error(s) (dcr 0x02ee) detected
3 torus receiver z- input pipe error(s) (dcr 0x02f1) detected
```

(a) before normalization

```
number torus receiver x input pipe error detected
number torus receiver x input pipe error detected
number register edram error detected
number register edram error detected
error receiving packet expecting type number
number torus receiver y input pipe error detected
number torus receiver z input pipe error detected
```

(b) after normalization

Figure 5.6.: Application of normalization on log records

Figure 5.6 exemplifies the effect of applying the normalization. Six example log messages from the Blue Gene/L log [OS07], used in the evaluation (Chapter 11), are shown in Figure 5.6a; the corresponding normalized messages are shown in Figure 5.6b. It is obvious that very similar log messages are mapped to the same normalized log message. This enables to programmatically grasp the semantic context of log messages as identical normalized log messages that are also mostly semantically identical.

5.5.1.2. Filtering

After the log is normalized by applying the aforementioned step, it can be processed by the filtering step, which removes redundant information. This section describes two types of filters used in this thesis, namely Adaptive Semantic Filtering and Duplicate Removal Filtering.

Adaptive Semantic Filter   Liang et al. [LZXS07a] propose a filtering algorithm, called Adaptive Semantic Filtering (ASF), which isolates important events in the Blue Gene/L log by removing redundant log entries. Log entries are considered redundant when they occur within a certain time frame and have a certain semantic correlation. The general idea behind ASF is that log records occurring close to each other in time most probably originate from the same root cause, even if the semantic correlation is not extraordinary high. On the other hand, log records with a larger time difference in between more probably originate from different root causes. Hence, the semantic correlation of two log records also needs to be higher in order to consider them to be redundant. To face this, ASF requires a higher semantic correlation of two log records if the time difference between them is greater than a certain threshold.

To calculate the semantic correlation between two log entries, the log messages are first normalized, as described in Section 5.5.1.1 and then transformed into dictionaries of words. As the dictionaries are simply boolean vectors, similarity coefficients such as the Phi correlation coefficient can be used to compute the correlation. We denote $c_{ab} \in \mathbb{N}_0$ with $a, b \in 0, 1$ as the number of words that are not present in any of the two log messages ($a = b = 0$), that are only present in the first log message ($a = 1, b = 0$), that are only present in the second log message ($a = 0, b = 1$) and that are present in both log messages ($a = b = 1$). The Phi correlation coefficient is then defined as [LZXS07a]:

$$
\phi = \frac{c_{00}c_{11} - c_{01}c_{10}}{\sqrt{(c_{00} + c_{01})(c_{10} + c_{11})(c_{00} + c_{10})(c_{01} + c_{11})}}
\tag{5.4}
$$

The formula yields similarity coefficients between -1 to 1. The more similar two log messages are (high c_{00} or high c_{11}), the closer the Phi correlation coefficient is to 1 and the more different two log messages are (high c_{01} or high c_{10}), the closer the Phi correlation coefficient is to -1. The two messages that have a high coefficient are reduced to only one even though they occur far apart from each other. On the other hand, two messages that are less similar may be reduced if they occur close to each other.

Duplicate Removal Filter A Duplicate Removal Filter (DRF) is a filter that we have developed based on a straightforward idea: the log messages that have the same information and occur within a certain time span can be reduced to only one log record. This removal step aims to decrease the computation complexity of the Phi correlation coefficient, while still maintaining a high classification quality.

5.5.2. System Event Classification

The information contained in the log files can be used to conclude about the current state of the system, whether the system is running normally or it is experiencing a problem. Although the log messages may have certain formats or patterns, they usually differ across different parts or different versions of the system. Furthermore, log files can grow very large in complex systems which makes manual classification infeasible.

Our event classification approach is based on supervised machine learning (Section 2.2.2) which takes a set of manually labeled log messages as input to the algorithm. The algorithm learns an internal model, e.g., decision trees, data clusters, and probabilistic representations, from the data by discovering the patterns of log messages and the relationship to the given labels. After the model is trained, it is used to classify log messages that are produced at runtime and tag them with a label.

Given the example in Figure 5.6a, the classification process starts by having a subset of the log manually labeled by the system administrators [OS07]. The labeled log is presented in Figure 5.7 where the labels are added to the beginning of the log messages. This example subset of log contains only two types of labels: "-" and "KERNREC" which implies that the machine learning model trained with this data will be able to classify and predict only two types of labels. At runtime, the unlabeled log messages are fed to the model which will classify them with the corresponding label.

To give a concrete example, Table 5.1 provides all labels contained in the Blue Gene/L log file, which is used in the evaluation, with examples of log messages and statistics about the number of occurrences in the data. The

```
- 4 torus receiver x+ input pipe error(s) (dcr 0x02ec) detected
- 1 torus receiver x- input pipe error(s) (dcr 0x02ed) detected
- 191790399 L3 EDRAM error(s) (dcr 0x0157) detected
- 2 L3 EDRAM error(s) (dcr 0x0157) detected
KERNREC Error receiving packet, expecting type 57
- 3 torus receiver y+ input pipe error(s) (dcr 0x02ee) detected
- 3 torus receiver z- input pipe error(s) (dcr 0x02f1) detected
```

Figure 5.7.: Example of labeled log messages

events that are classified in this stage will serve as a basis for predicting future events described in the next section.

5.5.3. System Event Prediction

The idea of event prediction is based on an assumption that patterns in the event log can lead to certain events in the near future. Unlike event classification, which aims to classify a log message with a label, event prediction looks at the current sequence of messages and tries to predict if any type of event will occur soon.

The training process of system event prediction starts by grouping a certain number of log messages from the past to the most recent one. Instead of taking the label of the current message for the training, we look ahead in time and take the label of the message in the future. However, predicting the occurrence of one label exactly at a specific time in the future is virtually impossible. This is because the predicted label may occur a few seconds earlier or later which makes our prediction a false positive. Therefore, we employ a prediction window where a prediction is regarded as correct if the predicted label occurs in this time window. Nonetheless, another issue remains in the consideration of the label as there can be many labels occurring in the prediction window. We solve this issue by dropping the type of the labels and consider a prediction as correct if there is at least a certain amount of any labels excluding "-" in that period.

Figure 5.8 illustrates the prediction approach. The parameters that can be adjusted for event prediction are the *number of past observations* to be taken into account, how long we look into the future (*lead time*), the *length*

5 | Component Failure Prediction

Count	Label	Message
1	KERNBIT	KERNEL FATAL ddr: redundant bit steering failed, sequencer timeout
1	KERNEXT	KERNEL FATAL external input interrupt (unit=0x03 bit=0x01): tree header with no target waiting
1	KERNTLBE	KERNEL FATAL instruction TLB error interrupt
1	MONILL	MONITOR FAILURE monitor caught java.lang.IllegalStateException: while executing CONTROL Operation
1	LINKBLL	LINKCARD FATAL MidplaneSwitchController::clearPort() bll_clear_port failed: R63-M0-L0-U19-A
2	MONNULL	MONITOR FAILURE While inserting monitor info into DB caught java.lang.NullPointerException
2	KERNFLOAT	KERNEL FATAL floating point unavailable interrupt
3	KERNRTSA	KERNEL FATAL rts assertion failed: personality->version == BGLPERSONALITY_VERSION in void start() at start.cc:131
3	MMCS	MMCS FATAL L3 major internal error
5	KERNPROG	KERNEL FATAL program interrupt
10	APPTORUS	APP FATAL external input interrupt (unit=0x02 bit=0x00): uncorrectable torus error
10	MASNORM	BGLMASTER FAILURE mmcs_server exited normally with exit code 13
12	MONPOW	MONITOR FAILURE monitor caught java.lang.UnsupportedOperationException: power module U69 not present and is stopping
14	KERNNOETH	KERNEL FATAL no ethernet link
14	LINKPAP	LINKCARD FATAL MidplaneSwitchController::parityAlignment() pap failed: R22-M0-L0-U22-D, status=00000000 00000000
16	KERNCON	LINKCARD FATAL MailboxMonitor::serviceMailboxes() lib_ido_error: -1033 BGLERR_IDO_PKT_TIMEOUT
18	KERNPAN	KERNEL FATAL kernel panic
24	LINKDISC	LINKCARD FATAL MidplaneSwitchController::sendTrain() port disconnected: R07-M1-L1-U19-E
37	MASABNORM	BGLMASTER FAILURE mmcs_server exited abnormally due to signal: Aborted
94	KERNSERV	KERNEL FATAL Power Good signal deactivated: R73-M1-NS, A service action may be required.
144	APPALLOC	APP FATAL ciod: Error creating node map from file /p/gb2/draeger/benchmark/dat16k_062205/map16k, bipartyz
166	LINKIAP	LINKCARD FATAL MidplaneSwitchController::receiveTrain() iap failed: R72-M1-L1-U18-A, status=beeaabff ec000000
192	KERNPOW	KERNEL FATAL Power deactivated: R05-M0-N4
209	KERNSOCK	KERNEL FATAL MailboxMonitor::serviceMailboxes() lib_ido_error: -1019 socket closed
320	APPCHILD	APP FATAL ciod: Error creating node map from file /p/gb2/cabot/miranda/newmaps/8k_128x64x1_8x4x4.map
342	KERNMC	KERNEL FATAL machine check interrupt
512	APPBUSY	APP FATAL ciod: Error creating node map from file /p/gb2/pakin1/sweep3d-5x5x400-10mk-3mmi-1024pes-sweep/sweep.map
720	KERNMINT	KERNEL FATAL Error: unable to mount filesystem
816	APPOUT	APP FATAL ciod: LOGIN chdir(/p/gb1/stella/RAPTOR/2183) failed: Input/output error
1503	KERNMICRO	KERNEL FATAL Microloader Assertion
1991	APPTO	APP FATAL ciod: Error reading message prefix on CioStream socket to 172.16.96.116:41739, Connection timed out
2048	APPUNAV	APP FATAL ciod: Error creating node map from file /home/auselton/bgl/64mps.sequential.mapfile
2370	APPRES	APP FATAL ciod: Error reading message prefix after LOAD_MESSAGE on CioStream socket to 172.16.96.116:52783
3983	KERNRTSP	KERNEL FATAL rts panic! - stopping execution
6145	APPREAD	APP FATAL ciod: failed to read message prefix on control stream CioStream socket to 172.16.96.116:33399
23338	KERNREC	KERNEL FATAL Error receiving packet on tree network, expecting type 57 instead of type 3
31531	KERNTERM	KERNEL FATAL rts: kernel terminated for reason 1004rts: bad message header
49651	KERNMNTF	KERNEL FATAL Lustre mount FAILED : bglio11 : block_id : location
63491	APPSEV	APP FATAL ciod: Error reading message prefix after LOGIN_MESSAGE on CioStream socket
152734	KERNSTOR	KERNEL FATAL data storage interrupt
4399503	KERNDTLB	KERNEL FATAL data TLB error interrupt
-		KERNEL INFO instruction cache parity error corrected

Table 5.1.: Statistics and example of log file collected from Blue Gene/L

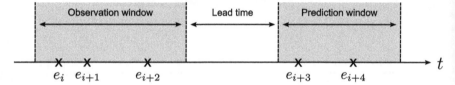

Figure 5.8.: Timeline of critical event prediction

```
4 torus receiver x+ input pipe error(s) (dcr 0x02ec) detected
1 torus receiver x- input pipe error(s) (dcr 0x02ed) detected
191790399 L3 EDRAM error(s) (dcr 0x0157) detected
```

(a) First group of log messages

```
1 torus receiver x- input pipe error(s) (dcr 0x02ed) detected
191790399 L3 EDRAM error(s) (dcr 0x0157) detected
2 L3 EDRAM error(s) (dcr 0x0157) detected
```

(b) Second group of log messages

Figure 5.9.: Example of grouped log messages

of the prediction window, and the percentage of the messages that have to be labeled with a fault state so that a failure should be predicted in this timeframe (*sensitivity*).

Using the example in Figure 5.6a for the illustration, the training phase groups a certain number of log messages together. Assume that the number of past observation is three, three consecutive log messages will be grouped as one entry. Figure 5.9a shows the first group of log messages. The next group of messages is obtained by sliding the observation window to the next message which is shown in Figure 5.9b.

As we are predicting whether there will be any label occurring in the near future, we neglect the label of those messages in the group and take the label of the future messages instead. Assume that the prediction window is two messages ahead in the future and contains two messages which are:

```
KERNREC Error receiving packet, expecting type 57
- 3 torus receiver y+ input pipe error(s) (dcr 0x02ee) detected
```

If we set the sensitivity to 50%, the first group of messages will be labeled as a "+" as it contains at least 50% of the messages not labeled with "-".

On the other hand, the prediction window of the second group of log messages will also slide to the next message and contain:

```
- 3 torus receiver y+ input pipe error(s) (dcr 0x02ee) detected
- 3 torus receiver z- input pipe error(s) (dcr 0x02f1) detected
```

The second group of messages will be labeled as a "-", as this prediction window does not contain any label other than "-".

This grouping process continues for the remaining part of the available log. When all log messages are processed, the grouped and labeled entries are used for training the model. At runtime, the new log messages are grouped according to the configured parameters and fed to the trained model which predicts the future event for that group.

5.6. Hard Drive Failure Prediction

This section describes the failure prediction approach to predict hard drive failures. The traditional method of predicting failures in hard drives is by using pre-defined thresholds on the S.M.A.R.T. parameters. Self-Monitoring, Analysis and Reporting Technology (S.M.A.R.T.) is an industry-standard hard disk drive technology embedded in the firmware which is being used in most modern hard drives [OP95]. During the drive's operation, its internal parameters, e.g., read/write error rate, servo, power-on time, and temperature, are recorded at regular intervals and can be accessed by the operating system. At runtime, if the value of one of the parameters exceeds the threshold, an alarm is raised. However, some parameters may not have direct effects on the pending failures. For example, the number of erroneous sectors may not represent the health of the drive if it remains constant and does not increase over time. Furthermore, a small variation of one parameter may not indicate a pending failure, but a certain pattern of many small variations may be a sign of a problem. For instance, a small increase of the number of bad sectors combined with a slightly longer read time may indicate a problem

Serial no.	Hours before failure	Temp1	FlyHeight1	Servo8	ReadError17	WriteError	⋯
100001	2.216	10	7962	0	0	57005	⋯
100001	2.200	12	7972	0	0	57005	⋯
100001	2.166	11	7949	0	8	57005	⋯
100001	2.133	9	7955	0	1280008	57005	⋯
⋮	⋮	⋮	⋮	⋮	⋮	⋮	⋯

Figure 5.10.: S.M.A.R.T. dataset example (excerpt)

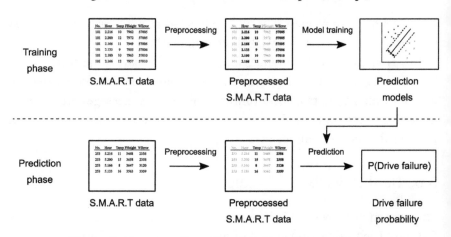

Figure 5.11.: Overview of hard drive failure prediction

although each individual parameter does not. This section describes how the S.M.A.R.T. data is preprocessed and used to predict hard drive failures.

Figure 5.10 shows an example S.M.A.R.T. dataset, which can be viewed as multiple streams of recorded parameters. Each row represents an observation which contains one monitored value for each parameter. These parameters are recorded until the drive experiences a problem and fails. These observations are used to create prediction models. The prediction models are used during the prediction phase to predict whether the drive is likely to fail in the near future. Figure 5.11 illustrates the overview of the approach.

5.6.1. Preprocessing

Before the learning algorithms are applied, the instances in the training set that represent failing and non-failing drives have to be separated so that they can be used to train different prediction models. However, if only the instances that were collected at the time of failures are used to train the failing model, this model will not be able to make predictions as it can recognize only the instances when the drives fail, not before they fail. Therefore, the instances that are collected before the failures should also be used to train the failing model. To determine how long this period should be, let us make two assumptions. First, we assume that the drive exhibits different characteristics throughout its life time. The prediction model that is trained with the instances collected from any operation period will be able to recognize them at runtime. Second, we assume that a sufficient warning time should be seven days before a drive fails. This will give system administrators enough time to prepare for the failure. As a result, the instances that were collected within seven days before the failures are grouped together, while those that are collected before seven days are collected in another group.

5.6.2. Predicting Hard Drive Failures

The failure prediction of hard drives is done by applying supervised machine learning techniques. The goal is to train the model to differentiate between the data that are collected from the healthy drives and the data that precede the failures. The data in the first group that were collected during the normal operation of the drive and do not precede any failures are used to create a model that represent a healthy drive. Those in the second group that occur before a drive failure or exactly when the drive fails are used to create a model that represent a failing drive. The created models are used at runtime to predict pending drive failures. The machine learning techniques described in Section 2.2.2 are applied to create prediction models from the S.M.A.R.T. dataset.

5.7. Summary

This chapter presents the component failure prediction which is the first step of the HORA approach and answers the research questions RQ1.1 and RQ1.2. In this chapter, the requirements for component failure predictors are presented. The component failure predictors based on three types of data, which are time series, event logs, and S.M.A.R.T. data, are introduced. These prediction techniques employ time series forecasting, machine learning and pattern recognition algorithms. Other prediction techniques, presented in Section 3.1, can also be applied in the HORA approach if they meet the stated requirements.

6

ARCHITECTURAL DEPENDENCY MODELING AND EXTRACTION

The HORA approach employs architectural models to represent the information regarding component dependencies required for predicting the propagation of failures. This chapter presents the model and how it can be extracted from the monitoring data and the existing architectural models.

Section 6.1 describes the research questions that will be answered in this chapter. Section 6.2 describes the information that is needed to represent architectural dependencies. Section 6.3 introduces HORA's Architectural Dependency Model (ADM), which is the model that contains architectural dependency information. Section 6.4 presents how an ADM can be created and extracted from existing architectural models. Section 6.5 summarizes the contribution of this chapter.

6.1. Research Questions

This chapter aims to answer the following research questions which have been previously stated in detail in Section 4.1:

- RQ2.1: Which architectural information can be used to improve online failure prediction?

- RQ2.2: How can the required architectural information for online failure prediction be modeled?

6.2. Architectural Dependency Information

Software systems are usually composed of a number of both hardware and software components. Hardware components are physical machines which include CPU, memory, hard drives, network interface, etc. These components have to function properly in order for the software components to work as designed. On the other hand, software components can be broken down to multiple sub-components depending on the perspectives. For example, from a service perspective, a software component can be internal services, such as business logic components, database, or third-party services. From a programming perspective, software components are classes and methods that are called and executed to complete a task.

The dependencies between these hardware and software components play an important role in how a failure propagates from one component to another. For instance, a CPU cannot continue to work if the memory is depleted. On the other hand, the software component deployed on the machine cannot function if the physical components are not working. Moreover, if one software component fails, either with a timing or content failure, the failure will propagate to the output interface. Other software components that depend on the failing component will receive an erroneous input which will also cause their results to be incorrect. The incorrect results then propagate through the control flow until it reaches the system boundary at which point the failure is visible to the users.

In this thesis, the connectors are not explicitly considered in the ADM. However, they can be included as a component that connects other components with each other. Furthermore, it is assumed that once a failure occurs in one component, it always propagates to the output interface. For example, if one component makes a call to a failing component, the failure will propagate and also cause a failure in the caller.

To be able to predict these cascading failures at runtime, the information regarding component dependencies is required. This information has to include 1) the dependency chain that specifies which components depend on which ones and 2) to which extent theses components rely on one another. The first piece of information lets us know how a failure of one component can propagate through multiple layers to other components in the system. The second piece of information allows us to estimate the effect of a component failure on other components and the whole service.

6.3. Architectural Dependency Model

There are already a number of existing architectural modeling languages and model extraction mechanisms [LMP08; SAG+06], e.g., PCM [BKR09], Descartes [BHK14] and SLAstic [Hoo14]. However, as previously stated in Section 2.3.3, these models are originally designed for different purposes. For instance, PCM focuses on predicting software performance and reliability at an early stage of the software development. Descartes aims at modeling the quality of service and resource management. SLAstic is designed for online capacity management of component-based software systems. Although they contain architectural information of the system, the information regarding how a failure of one component can affect the others is not explicitly represented. Thus, we introduce ADM which aims at being an intermediate model representing only the architectural dependencies and how failures propagate between components.

The Architectural Dependency Model (ADM) lists software and hardware components along with the dependencies between them. The dependencies indicate the relationship between components according to the architectural configuration (Section 2.3.1), e.g., calling relationships of software components or deployments of software components on hardware components. Each dependency is annotated with a degree of dependency, or dependency weight. A dependency weight represents how much one component requires another component to function correctly. In other words, it is the probability that a failure of one component will affect another one. A degree of dependency is assigned to a pair of components with a direct dependency as a probability. This probability represents the likelihood that a component fails because another component that it requires fails.

An ADM can be formally defined as a set $E = \{e_1, e_2, \ldots, e_n\}$ where n is the number of components. Each element e is a pair $\langle C, D \rangle$ where

- C is a software or hardware component or sub-component that provides a service either internally to other components, or externally to other systems or users

- $D = \{d_1, d_2, \ldots, d_n\}$ where each element d is a pair $\langle C^r, w \rangle$ with

    - C^r is the required component

    - w is the corresponding dependency weight to C^r

Table 6.1 shows an example of an ADM in a table representation. The first column lists all components in the system and the second column lists their dependencies. Each dependency is a pair representing the dependent component and the corresponding weight. The weight indicates the probability that a failure of the dependent component will affect the required component. For instance, component C_i has two dependencies. The first dependency is to component C_j with the weight $w_{C_i C_j}$. The second dependency is to component C_k with the weight $w_{C_i C_k}$. In this case, the component C_i is called a requiring component and the component C_j and C_k are called required components. In the same manner, C_j and C_k can also have dependencies to other components as well.

Component	Required components and weights
C_i	$\{(C_j, w_{C_iC_j}), (C_k, w_{C_iC_k})\}$
C_j	$\{(C_k, w_{C_k})\}$
C_k	$\{\ldots\}$
...	...

Table 6.1.: Table representation of an ADM

6.4. Extraction of an Architectural Dependency Model

The ADM can be created manually by system experts or extracted automatically from the existing architectural models. Section 6.4.1 presents a way to manually create an ADM. Section 6.4.2 presents the concept of an automated extraction of an ADM based on the architectural knowledge. Section 6.4.3 presents a transformation from a SLAstic model to an ADM. Section 6.4.4 presents an extraction of an ADM directly from Kieker monitoring data.

6.4.1. Manual Creation of Architectural Dependency Model

A straightforward way to identify component dependencies is by manually specifying them. System experts, for example, software architects, developers, or system administrators, who have knowledge regarding the structure and behavior of the system can identify components and their dependencies.

Figure 6.1 illustrates *Running Example 2* that contains four software components with calling dependencies. From the architecture, it can be observed that component A and B depend on component C. On the other hand, component C depends on component D. In this example, a failure of D can cause C to fail which, consequently, can cause A and B to fail. The ADM of *Running Example 2* is shown in Table 6.2. The dependency weight in the ADM can be interpreted as the component's failure probability when an adjacent component in the dependency chain fails. For example, component A and B will fail with a probability of 1.0 if component C fails. In the same manner, component C will fail with a probability of 1.0 if component D fails. Component D does not have any dependency and therefore cannot be

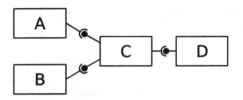

Figure 6.1.: *Running Example 2*: component diagram

Component	Required components and weights
A	{(C, 1.0)}
B	{(C, 1.0)}
C	{(D, 1.0)}
D	{}

Table 6.2.: Table representation of the ADM for *Running Example 2*

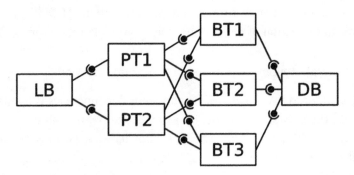

Figure 6.2.: *Running Example 1*: component diagram

affected by the failure of other components.

As a more realistic example, Figure 6.2 depicts a component diagram of the three-tier application previously presented in Figure 1.1 (Page 4). The application contains four types of components; load balancer (LB), presentation tier (PT), business tier (BT), and data tier (DB). Each of the layers can be scaled horizontally (scale out or scale in) depending on the workload. In this example, the presentation tier is scaled out to two instances and the business tier is scaled out to three instances.

The component dependencies listed here can be specified by a system expert. The dependency weights can be determined based on the architecture of the system which assumes that the requests of each service in each layer are equally load-balanced to the next layer.

Table 6.3 shows the table representation of the ADM. Following a topological order, the database (DB) has no dependencies to other components; the business-tier instances BT1–3 depend on DB; the presentation-tier instances PT1–2 depend on the business-tier instances BT1–3; and the load balancer depends on PT1–2. Additionally, Table 6.3 includes the weights associated to these dependencies—in this case, assuming that requests among the tiers are equally load-balanced to the instances of the next tier. In this example, if one of the presentation-tier instances fails, the probability of the load balancer failing increases by 0.5. If both PT1 and PT2 fail, the probability becomes 1.0 which implies that the load balancer will also definitely fail. On the other hand, the requests from presentation-tier instances are equally forwarded to three business-tier instances. This implies that the failure probability of a presentation-tier instance increases by approximately 0.33 for each business-tier instance failure.

The ADM shown here is created by manually analyzing the architecture of the system. Note that for the sake of simplicity, we consider the six nodes from the example as monolithic components. For realistic scenarios, these components can be further decomposed into software and hardware components with measures, such as service response time, method execution time, or resource utilization. In other words, the entities in the ADM do not necessarily have to be components but can be sub-component entities and their measures that represent their statuses. For example, a software component may provide more than one service that is fulfilled by many functions. A failure of one function may contribute to a partial failure of the service. Thus, the use of sub-component measures, such as method response time and resource utilization, to represent components in the ADM allows a more fine-grained modeling of the architectural dependencies.

Although the manual creation of an ADM may be applicable for small-scale systems with a small number of components, manually specifying

Component	Required components and weights
DB	{}
BT1	{(DB, 1.0)}
BT2	{(DB, 1.0)}
BT3	{(DB, 1.0)}
PT1	{(BT1, 0.3$\overline{3}$), (BT2, 0.3$\overline{3}$), (BT3, 0.3$\overline{3}$)}
PT2	{(BT1, 0.3$\overline{3}$), (BT2, 0.3$\overline{3}$), (BT3, 0.3$\overline{3}$)}
LB	{(PT1, 0.5), (PT2, 0.5)}

Table 6.3.: Table representation of the ADM for *Running Example 1*

dependencies of large systems can be error-prone and time-consuming. Moreover, for fast-evolving systems, of which the architecture continuously changes over time, manual creation of the ADM cannot be achieved in a timely manner.

6.4.2. Automated Extraction of Architectural Dependency Model

Automated extraction of the ADM is carried out by means of a form of data structures, e.g., architectural models, that provide information regarding the system's structure and behavior. This information can be obtained either from static or dynamic program analysis.

Static program analysis [CE09; Lou06] is performed to obtain software behavior, e.g., architecture, correctness, safety, without executing the application. An example of static program analysis is source code analysis which has an advantage that it can be done without deploying the system in a real environment. However, since the behavior of the system can be influenced by the workload, i.e., different types of requests can invoke different functionalities of the system, the resulting architectural model of static analysis usually does not include such information, e.g., how often a component calls the others. For example, for an online shopping website, if a user does not store a payment method in the system, the website would redirect him or her to another page that asks for this information. Thus, static analysis based on the source code can provide only the dependency chains between components, i.e., which components are connected to which ones. The dependency weights that indicate to which extent a failure of one component will affect the others are not present.

On the other hand, *dynamic program analysis* [GS14], is performed by analyzing a running system. One method of dynamic analysis is software instrumentation where modifications are made to the software to obtain the required data. Monitoring traces are one of the data which contain information regarding runtime behavior of the system [Hoo14; LMP08], e.g., method response times and calling relationships. From this information, the dependency weights between components can be computed.

In this thesis, the application is instrumented using Kieker [HWH12]. These traces are then analyzed to create an architectural model. The architectural model used as the source is the SLAstic model [Hoo14] which contains information regarding the structure and behavior of the system, and can be automatically extracted from Kieker monitoring data.

The monitoring data required for the automated model extraction has to contain system-level resource usage, e.g., CPU utilization, and detailed execution traces of the application for each user request. From this data, the hardware and software components are discovered and linked together according to their relationships. The result of this automated extraction is a SLAstic model [Hoo14] which includes software components and their relationships, deployment information, and number of invocations of each component. By combining the information from the SLAstic model, we obtain sufficient knowledge about the dependencies of the components to create an ADM.

Figure 6.3 depicts the overview of the automated extraction of the ADM. At runtime, the system is monitored and the monitoring data is collected. Architectural models, e.g., SLAstic, can be extracted from the monitoring data. These architectural models can be transformed into an ADM. Nonetheless, an ADM can also be extracted directly from the monitoring data. The ADM extracted directly from the monitoring data and the one transformed from the architectural model are equivalent since the algorithms are based on the same concept, which will be described in the next subsections.

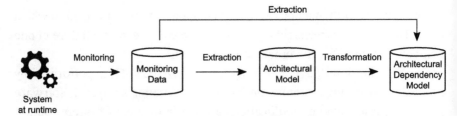

Figure 6.3.: Overview of automated extraction of the ADM

The following subsections describe the concept of how the dependencies between different types of components can be extracted from the architectural knowledge and how the dependency weights can be computed for each component. Sections 6.4.2.1 to 6.4.2.3 present how dependencies between software components, hardware components, and software and hardware components, respectively, are extracted.

6.4.2.1. Dependencies Between Software Components

Software components are classes, methods, or third-party services that work with each other to fulfill the required functionality of the software. For example, a successful execution of one method can depend on many other methods depending on the call graph.

There are two approaches to extract the information regarding the software components and their dependencies from the architectural models; analyzing the architecture of the system and analyzing the calling relationships between components. The following sections describe these approaches in detail.

Analyzing Architectural Structure   This approach of extraction is relatively straightforward and is based on an assumption that the invocations between components, e.g., between software components or between architectural layers, are equally load-balanced to all instances in the next layer. For example, in a scalable system where each type of component can be

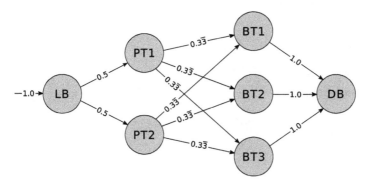

Figure 6.4.: Degrees of dependencies of *Running Example 1* extracted by analyzing architectural structure

scaled horizontally, the calls to this type of component will be distributed to each of the instances equally. In practice, this type of load-balancing strategy is called round-robin load balancing since all back-end components are called in a round-robin fashion.

The degree of dependency or dependency weight, denoted by w, between any two software components C_i and C_j in adjacent layers can be computed as

$$w_{C_i C_j} = \frac{1}{n_{C_i}} \tag{6.1}$$

where n_{C_i} is the number of instances of the next layer that are directly connected to component C_i.

Figure 6.4 illustrates the degrees of dependency of *Running Example 1* (Figure 1.1) extracted using this method. The system is a three-tier application containing a load balancer, a presentation tier, a business tier, and a database tier. The degrees of dependencies from an instance in one layer to the instances in the next layer are the same and sum up to 1.0. For example, the degrees of dependencies of LB to PT1 and PT2 are 0.5 and those of PT1 to all three BTs are $0.3\overline{3}$. The resulting ADM of this approach is similar to that of the manual creation approach presented in the previous section (Section 6.4.1).

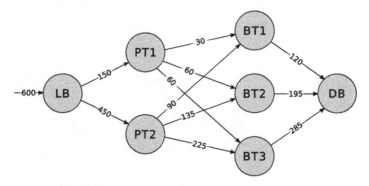

Figure 6.5.: Example of calling relationship and number of invocations (denoted by arrows and the corresponding numbers) of *Running Example 1* extracted from the SLAstic model

Analyzing Calling Relationships Although the previous method is simple and straightforward, in practice, the number of invocations to the next layer do not have to be equally distributed to all instances. The distribution can depend on many factors, e.g., the configuration of the load balancing strategy or the capacity of each instance at runtime. For instance, some nodes may have more computational power while some may have more memory or disk space. Therefore, the ADM extraction based only on the structure of the system may not represent the true behavior of the system.

Figure 6.5 visualizes an example of calling relationships as a diagram showing the number of invocations between components. The invocations between layers are not equally distributed to the next layer. In order to compute the degrees of dependencies, the numbers of invocations can be used to represent how one component depends on the others. For example, the higher the number of invocations, the higher the dependency between the caller and the callee.

The degree of dependency between two software components A and B can be computed based on the numbers of invocations as

$$w_{C_i C_j} = \frac{v_{C_i C_j}}{\sum_{k=1}^{n} v_{C_k C_i}} \qquad (6.2)$$

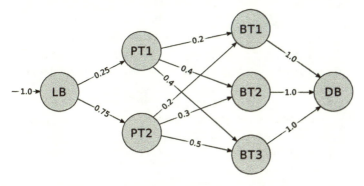

Figure 6.6.: Degrees of dependencies of *Running Example 1* extracted by analyzing calling relationship

where $v_{C_i C_j}$ is the number of invocations from component C_i to component C_j, $v_{C_k C_i}$ is the number of invocations from component C_k to component C_i, and n is the total number of components in the system.

In Figure 6.5, LB is invoked 600 times and PT1 is invoked by LB 150 times. Thus, the degree of dependency between LB and PT1 is $\frac{150}{600} = 0.25$. This implies that if PT1 fails, the probability of LB failing is 0.25. The degree of dependencies of other components can be computed in the same manner. Figure 6.6 shows the degrees of dependencies between components computed by using the calling relationship.

In this example, it can be observed that the sum of the outgoing dependency weights is equal to 1.0. This is because the request from one tier is load-balanced to the instances in the next tier. Thus, only one instance in the next tier is invoked per one invocation of the previous tier. However, this is not always the case. Figure 6.7 illustrates a simple example of a software component that requires three other software components. When componentA is invoked, componentB, componentC, and componentD are invoked once. For example, if componentA is invoked 100 times, the other three will also be invoked 100 times each. Hence, the number of invocations of componentA is equal to those of the other components. The numerator and the denominator of Equation 6.2 become the same value. As a result,

```
public class ComponentA {
  Component componentB = new ComponentB();
  Component componentC = new ComponentC();
  Component componentD = new ComponentD();

  public void compute() {
    componentB.compute();
    componentC.compute();
    componentD.compute();
  }
}
```

Figure 6.7.: A simple example of a software component with outgoing dependency weights of 1.0

the dependency weights from componentA to each of the callees will be 1.0.

The extraction of dependency weights between software components by analyzing calling relationships considers the dependencies emerged from the control flow. Although the presented example illustrates a simple scenario in which the calls are made sequentially, the loops and branches are also considered in the extraction of the ADM. If there is a branch that results in an additional call to another component, the control flow will indicate that there is a branch. The extraction algorithm will be able to detect this branch in the control flow and create a dependency to the called component. If there is a loop that causes a component to make many calls to another component, the number of invocations between them will increase. The dependency weight of these two component will also increase based on the number of invocations.

6.4.2.2. Dependencies Between Hardware Components

A physical machine is composed of various types of hardware that need to work together properly to run the software, e.g., CPU, memory, or hard drive. A failure of one component can lead to the failures of other components.

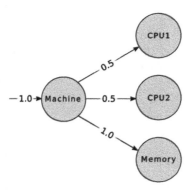

Figure 6.8.: Degree of dependency between hardware components

For example, a server may slow down if the memory is exhausted due to memory swapping or if the CPU is overutilized.

The HORA approach models the hardware components as parts of the whole machine. The failure of one hardware component can definitely cause the whole machine to fail. The degree of dependency from the machine to each component is, thus, 1.0. In the cases where the machine is equipped with multiple CPUs, the failure of one CPU does not necessarily have to cause a failure to the whole machine. Thus, the degree of dependency to each CPU, $w_{C_m C_c}$ is computed as

$$w_{C_m C_c} = \frac{1}{n_{CPU}} \tag{6.3}$$

where C_m is the machine, C_c is the CPU, and n_{CPU} is the total number of cores. For example, the degree of dependency of the machine to each CPU core in a dual core CPU is 0.5. Figure 6.8 illustrates this concept where one machine is composed of a dual core CPU and memory.

6.4.2.3. Dependencies Between Software and Hardware Components

In addition to the dependencies between software components or those between hardware components, there are also dependencies between software

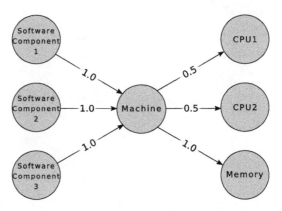

Figure 6.9.: Degree of dependency between software and hardware components

and hardware components. The software components that are deployed on a physical node require that the hardware components of that node operate correctly. If the machine fails, the software will also fail. Thus, the degree of dependency of each software component to the machine on which it is deployed becomes 1.0.

Figure 6.9 depicts an example of the ADM with dependencies between software and hardware components. There are three software components that are deployed on the same physical machine which is composed of different hardware components, e.g., CPU and memory. If these hardware components fail, the software components that are deployed on this machine will also fail.

In addition to actual hardware components, virtual hardware components, i.e., virtual machines, can also be modeled in a similar manner. Software components that are deployed on a virtual machine are not aware that the machine is not physical. If the virtual machine fails, the software components will also fail. However, a virtual machine also depends on a physical machine. The virtual hardware components require physical hardware components to function. Thus, a virtual CPU would have a dependency of 1.0 to the physical CPU, while a virtual memory would also have a dependency of 1.0 to the physical memory.

6 | Architectural Dependency Modeling and Extraction

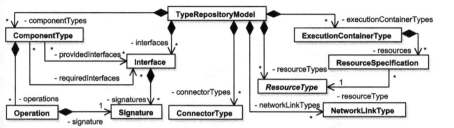

Figure 6.10.: An excerpt of the meta-model for the type repository [Hoo14]

6.4.3. Transformation From SLAstic To ADM

In the previous section (Section 6.4.2), the concept of an automated extraction of an ADM using architectural knowledge is presented. This section presents the SLAstic metamodels including the extension to the models and the extension to the extraction algorithm that produces the ADM.

The transformation from a SLAstic model to an ADM requires both structural and behavioral information. This information is already present in the SLAstic model. The structural information is obtained from the type repository, component assembly, component deployment, and execution environment model. The type repository, depicted in Figure 6.10, provides information regarding which types of software components implement which operations. Specifically, it is provided by the Operation, Signature, and Interface classes. Furthermore, the ExecutionContainerType, ResourceSpecification, and ResourceType classes provide the specifications of the execution containers. The information regarding how assembly components are connected is provided by the AssemblyComponent and Interface classes in the component assembly model illustrated in Figure 6.11. The component deployment model describes how components are deployed in the execution environment as depicted in Figure 6.12. The execution environment model provides the information regarding the execution containers and the network links as shown in Figure 6.13.

The dependencies and dependency weights between software components in ADM are obtained by analyzing the number of invocations between

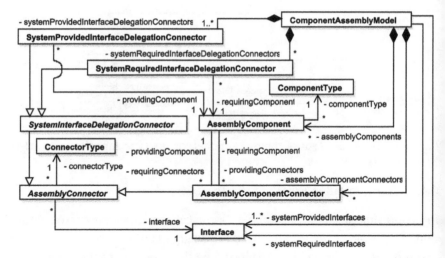

Figure 6.11.: An excerpt of the meta-model for the component assembly [Hoo14]

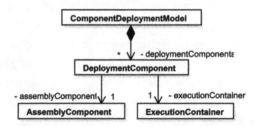

Figure 6.12.: The meta-model for the component deployment [Hoo14]

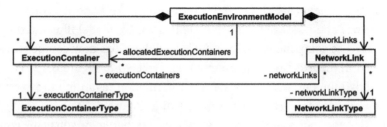

Figure 6.13.: The meta-model for the execution environment [Hoo14]

components, as previously described in Section 6.4.2. This information is obtained directly from the usage model, as depicted in Figure 6.14, which contains information about the calls to operations and interfaces. `CallingRelationship` records the information about a call by storing the following information:

- `Operation`, which is the caller
- `Signature`, which is the signature of the callee,
- `Interface`, which is the interface of the callee, and
- `FrequencyDistribution`, which is the histogram describing the behavior of the calls, e.g., how many calls have been made to this callee.

However, the usage model stores only the calling information on the assembly level, which is the information of which type of components call which type of components. The missing information on the deployment level creates a problem when there are multiple instances of a component type deployed in the system. The number of invocations of each individual deployment component is lost and their actual behavior, i.e., number of invocations, cannot be obtained.

In order to retrieve detailed calling information on the deployment level, the meta-model of SLAstic has to be extended. Figure 6.14 depicts the extended meta-model of SLAstic usage model. The meta-model is extended to include the following components:

- `DeploymentOperationCallFrequency`, which is a sub-class of `OperationCallFrequency` and stores the number of invocations of a component on the deployment level,
- `DeploymentCallingRelationship`, which is a sub-class of `CallingRelationship` and stores the calling information, i.e., which deployment component calls which deployment component, and
- `DeploymentComponent`, which is the called deployment component.

In addition to the extension to the model, the extraction algorithm from monitoring data to the SLAstic model is also extended. The extension takes

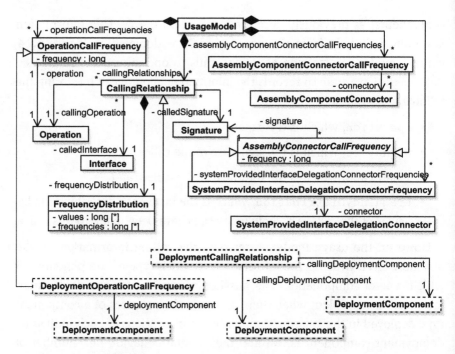

Figure 6.14.: The meta-model for the usage model [Hoo14] and the extensions denoted by dashed boxes

into account the calling information on the deployment level that is present in the monitoring data. The resulting SLAstic model, thus, contains all the information required for HORA to extract the dependencies and create an ADM.

Algorithm 6.1 illustrates the transformation from a SLAstic model to an ADM. The algorithm first iterates through all DeploymentCalling-Relationships and obtains the caller and callee of all internal and external calls. It then extracts the number of calls that has been made from a specific caller to a specific callee. After all calling relationships are extracted, the normalization is done on the number of calls to obtain the dependency weights. This normalization process is done as described in Section 6.4.2.1. The dependencies of the caller to hardware components are computed as described in Section 6.4.2.3. The dependencies between hardware components are computed as described in Section 6.4.2.2. The result of this transformation is an ADM which represents the dependencies between components with the corresponding dependency weights.

Algorithm 6.1 Transformation From SLAstic To ADM

Require: SLAstic model
 1: Extract `DeploymentCallingRelationships` from SLAstic model
 2: Initialize count of all callers to all callees to 0
 3: **for all** calling relationship R in `DeploymentCallingRelationships` **do**
 4:     Extract caller C_i and callee C_j from R
 5:     Increment count for the call between C_i and C_j
 6: **end for**
 7: **for all** caller C_i in callers **do**
 8:     Retrieve the number of invocations from any component to C_i
 9:     **for all** callee C_j in callees invoked by C_i **do**
10:         Retrieve number of calls from C_i to C_j
11:         Normalize number of calls to 0.0–1.0
12:         Store dependency from C_i to C_j and normalized value in ADM
13:     **end for**
14: **end for**
15: **for all** deployment component D in `DeploymentComponents` **do**
16:     Retrieve execution container E of D from SLAstic model
17:     Store dependency from D to E and weight of 1.0 in ADM
18: **end for**
19: Extract `ExecutionContainers` from SLAstic model
20: **for all** execution container E in `ExecutionContainers` **do**
21:     **for all** CPU P in `ExecutionContainers` **do**
22:         Store dependency from E to P and weight of $1/n_{CPU}$ in ADM
23:     **end for**
24:     Store dependency from E to memory and weight of 1.0 in ADM
25: **end for**
26: **return** ADM

6.4.4. Extraction of ADM From Kieker Monitoring Data

The extraction of an ADM from monitoring data is similar to the extraction of a SLAstic model via dynamic analysis [Hoo14, p. 150]. However, as ADM contains only information regarding dependencies between components, the extraction is more straightforward than that for the SLAstic model.

Algorithm 6.2 Extraction of ADM From Kieker Monitoring Data

Require: Kieker monitoring data
1: Group OperationExecutions by traceID
2: **for all** traceID in traceIDs **do**
3:     Order OperationExecutions by EOI and ESS
4:     **for all** operation execution O in OperationExecutions **do**
5:         Extract caller C_i from O
6:         Extract callee C_j from the next operation execution
7:         Increment count for the call between C_i and C_j
8:         Extract execution container E of C_i from O
9:         Store dependency from C_i to E and weight of 1.0 in ADM
10:     **end for**
11: **end for**
12: **for all** caller C_i in callers **do**
13:     Retrieve the number of invocations from any component to C_i
14:     **for all** callee C_j in callees invoked by C_i **do**
15:         Retrieve number of calls from C_i to C_j
16:         Normalize number of calls to 0.0–1.0
17:         Store dependency from C_i to C_j and normalized value in ADM
18:     **end for**
19: **end for**
20: **for all** execution container E in ADM **do**
21:     **for all** CPU P in ExecutionContainers **do**
22:         Store dependency from E to P and weight of $1/n_{CPU}$ in ADM
23:     **end for**
24:     Store dependency from E to memory and weight of 1.0 in ADM
25: **end for**
26: **return** ADM

Algorithm 6.2 illustrates the extraction of an ADM from Kieker monitoring data. The input of the extraction is Kieker monitoring data. This data is a stream of OperationExecutions which contains the control flow information of the application. In the first step, the OperationExecutions are split into groups according to the traceID and sorted by the EOI and ESS values (Section 2.3.5.2). Then, for each control flow with the same traceID, the number of invocations between callers and callees is counted. The normalization process is carried out similar to that of the transformation from SLAstic to ADM described in the previous section (Section 6.4.3). However, instead of obtaining the information regarding the execution container from the SLAstic model, this information is obtained directly from the OperationExecution. As previously described in Section 2.3.5.2, each OperationExecution contains the hostname of the machine on which the operation is deployed and executed. This information is used to create the dependencies from the operations to the corresponding execution containers.

6.5. Summary

This chapter presents the Architectural Dependency Model (ADM) which is the second step of the HORA approach and provides answers to the research questions RQ2.1 and RQ2.2. In this chapter, the information required for capturing the architectural dependencies is presented and the ADM, which is the model that represents the dependencies between components in the system, is introduced. The concepts of the manual and automated extraction of the ADM based on the architectural knowledge are presented. Furthermore, the transformation of the ADM from the SLAstic model and the extraction from the Kieker monitoring data are also presented.

7

FAILURE PROPAGATION MODELING AND PREDICTION

The Architectural Dependency Model (ADM), introduced in Chapter 6, represents the architecture of the system with component dependencies and the corresponding weights. However, the ADM is not suitable for failure prediction because the probabilities of cascading failures are not explicitly included.

Section 7.1 describes the research question that will be answered in this chapter. Section 7.2 introduces HORA's Failure Propagation Model (FPM) which is the representation that is suitable for predicting cascading failures. Section 7.3 presents the transformation from an ADM to an FPM. Section 7.4 presents how the model is kept alive at runtime. Section 7.5 presents the inference of the FPM. Section 7.6 summarizes the contribution of this chapter.

7.1. Research Question

This chapter aims to answer the following research question which has been previously stated in detail in Section 4.1:

- RQ3.1: What is a suitable model to represent the combined information?

7.2. Failure Propagation Model

A Failure Propagation Model (FPM) is an abstraction that represents the concept of a model that can infer failure propagations. In this work, the FPM employs the formalism of Bayesian networks [Bis06], introduced in Section 2.2.3, which is a probabilistic directed acyclic graph that can represent random variables and their conditional dependencies. The FPM allows to infer the failure probabilities of components in the dependency chain when other components in the chain are failing.

Based on *Running Example 2* in Figure 6.1 (Page 104), the extracted ADM indicates the probabilities of a component failure if its adjacent component fails. However, it does not provide the failure probability if a non-adjacent component, i.e., component in the dependency chain, fails. The FPM allows this using Bayesian inference as described in Section 2.2.3. The FPM of *Running Example 2* is illustrated in Figure 7.1. The nodes represent the components while the edges represent the direction of the failure propagation. For example, it can be interpreted that the failure of component D can cause component C to fail. On the other hand, the failure of component C can cause component A and B to fail.

For each node in the Bayesian network, there is a Condition Probability Table (CPT) which lists marginal probability of that variable with respect to the others. Table 7.1 shows the CPTs of the components in Figure 7.1. Component D, which does not depend on any other component, has the simplest CPT shown in Table 7.1d. Its failure probability is affected only by itself. Therefore, its CPT contains only one row which indicates the probability of component D failing ($P(D_F)$) and not failing ($1 - P(D_F)$). Component

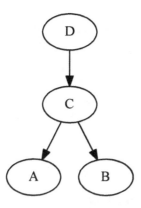

Figure 7.1.: FPM of *Running Example 2* in Figure 6.1

C fails	A fails	
	True	False
False	$P(C_F)$	$1 - P(C_F)$
True	1.0	0.0

(a) CPT of Component A

C fails	B fails	
	True	False
False	$P(C_F)$	$1 - P(C_F)$
True	1.0	0.0

(b) CPT of Component B

D fails	C fails	
	True	False
False	$P(D_F)$	$1 - P(D_F)$
True	1.0	0.0

(c) CPT of Component C

D fails	
True	False
$P(D_F)$	$1 - P(D_F)$

(d) CPT of Component D

Table 7.1.: CPTs of *Running Example 2*

A, B, and C all depend on one other component, so, their CPTs contain one additional column which indicate the health status of the component they depend on. Each row of the table represents the failure probability if the required component fails. In the case of component A, for example, if component C fails, component A will also fail. Thus, the probability is 1.0, as shown in the second row of Table 7.1a ('C fails' is true). If component C is functioning correctly, the failure probability of component A is affected by A itself, as shown in the first row ('C fails' is false).

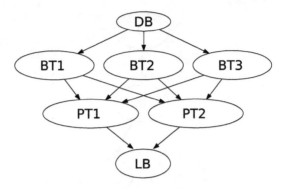

Figure 7.2.: FPM of *Running Example 1* in Figure 6.2

Figure 7.2 depicts the FPM for *Running Example 1*. For simplicity reasons, in this example we only consider each physical machine as a node in the graph without going into the details of each machine, e.g., software sub-components or hardware components.

The conditional dependencies between the nodes in the graph are represented by CPTs. Each node in the graph has a corresponding CPT which contains conditional probabilities of possible failures occurring, given the failure probability of its parent components. For instance, the database is a node that does not depend on any other nodes. Therefore, its CPT contains only two failure probabilities that represent the probability of a failure occurring, and not occurring, in the database itself. The table is shown in Table 7.2a. The failure probability is denoted by $P(\text{DB}_F)$ which is computed at runtime by the corresponding component failure predictor, as detailed in Chapter 5. On the other hand, the operation of a business tier (BT1–3) requires a database (DB) with a dependency weight of 1.0, according to the ADM in Table 6.3. This means that if the database fails, the business-tier instances will also fail. The CPT of the business-tier instance BT1 is presented in Table 7.2b. The first row indicates the failure probability of the business tier itself, if the database is operating properly. The second row indicates the probability of BT1 failing if the database fails.

DB fails	
True	False
$P(DB_F)$	$1 - P(DB_F)$

(a) CPT of DB

DB fails	BT1 fails	
	True	False
False	$P(BT1_F)$	$1 - P(BT1_F)$
True	1.0	0.0

(b) CPT of BT1

BT1 fails	BT2 fails	BT3 fails	PT1 fails	
			True	False
False	False	False	$P(PT1_F)$	$1 - P(PT1_F)$
False	False	True	$0.3\overline{3}$	$0.6\overline{6}$
False	True	False	$0.3\overline{3}$	$0.6\overline{6}$
False	True	True	$0.6\overline{6}$	$0.3\overline{3}$
True	False	False	$0.3\overline{3}$	$0.6\overline{6}$
True	False	True	$0.6\overline{6}$	$0.3\overline{3}$
True	True	False	$0.6\overline{6}$	$0.3\overline{3}$
True	True	True	1.0	0.0

(c) CPT of PT1

PT1 fails	PT2 fails	LB fails	
		True	False
False	False	$P(LB_F)$	$1 - P(LB_F)$
False	True	0.5	0.5
True	False	0.5	0.5
True	True	1.0	0.0

(d) CPT of LB

Table 7.2.: Selected CPTs of *Running Example 1* in Figure 6.2

A more complex relationship can be seen in the presentation tier which requires at least one business-tier instance. If one business-tier instance fails, the presentation tier can still operate by forwarding requests to the remaining business-tier instances. As listed in Table 6.3, the dependency weight of each presentation-tier instance to each business-tier instance is approximately $0.3\overline{3}$. This implies that, for each business tier failure, the failure probability of the presentation-tier instances will increase by approximately $0.3\overline{3}$. Hence, if all business-tier instances fail, this failure probability will sum up to 1.0 which means that the presentation-tier instances will also fail. The CPT of PT1 is presented in Table 7.2c.

The CPT of the load balancer is shown in Table 7.2d. The availability of the load balancer represents the availability of the whole service because if the load balancer fails, users can no longer access the service. Since the load balancer forwards the requests to the two instances of the presentation tier, the CPT, thus, contains the dependency to those components. Given that the load balancer is healthy, if one of the presentation-tier instances fails, the probability of the load balancer failing becomes 0.5. If both of them fail, the failure probability becomes 1.0.

7.3. Transformation From ADM To FPM

The transformation of an ADM to an FPM allows the inference of the failure propagation that is not possible with the ADM. To deduce this information from the model, all dependencies of the components need to be taken into account. This section details how this transformation can be achieved.

Assuming that a component c_0 depends on n other components with $n \geq 1$, the CPT of a component c_0 can be expressed by a multiplication of a truth table matrix $\mathbf{T}$ of size $2^n \times n$ and the weight matrix $\mathbf{W}_{c_0}$ of size $n \times 2$ and can be written as

$$\text{CPT}_{c_0} = \mathbf{T}_{c_0} \cdot \mathbf{W}_{c_0} \tag{7.1}$$

where

$$
\mathbf{T}_{c_0} = \begin{pmatrix}
 & c_1 & \cdots & c_{n-2} & c_{n-1} & c_n \\
 & 0 & \cdots & 0 & 0 & 0 \\
 & 0 & \cdots & 0 & 0 & 1 \\
 & 0 & \cdots & 0 & 1 & 0 \\
 & 0 & \cdots & 0 & 1 & 1 \\
 & \vdots & \ddots & \vdots & \vdots & \vdots \\
 & 1 & \cdots & 1 & 1 & 1
\end{pmatrix}, \tag{7.2}
$$

$$
\mathbf{W}_{c_0} = \begin{pmatrix}
w_{c_0 c_1} & 1 - w_{c_0 c_1} \\
w_{c_0 c_2} & 1 - w_{c_0 c_2} \\
\vdots & \vdots \\
w_{c_0 c_n} & 1 - w_{c_0 c_n}
\end{pmatrix}, \tag{7.3}
$$

with $c_i, 1 \le i \le n$, are required components and $w_{c_0 c_i}$ are the corresponding dependency weights from component c_0 to component c_i. This creates a matrix of size $2^n \times 2$ which is the CPT of the component.

Let us consider the component PT1 in *Running Example 1* in Figure 6.2 as an example. In this example, PT1 depends on three other components, which are BT1, BT2, and BT3. The truth table matrix $\mathbf{T}_{BT1}$ can be written as

$$
\mathbf{T}_{PT1} = \begin{pmatrix}
BT1 & BT2 & BT3 \\
0 & 0 & 0 \\
0 & 0 & 1 \\
0 & 1 & 0 \\
0 & 1 & 1 \\
1 & 0 & 0 \\
1 & 0 & 1 \\
1 & 1 & 0 \\
1 & 1 & 1
\end{pmatrix} \tag{7.4}
$$

and the weight matrix **W** can be obtained from the ADM in Table 6.3 which can be written as

$$\mathbf{W}_{PT1} = \begin{pmatrix} w_{PT1 \to BT1} & 1 - w_{PT1 \to BT1} \\ w_{PT1 \to BT2} & 1 - w_{PT1 \to BT2} \\ w_{PT1 \to BT3} & 1 - w_{PT1 \to BT3} \end{pmatrix} = \begin{pmatrix} 0.3\overline{3} & 0.6\overline{6} \\ 0.3\overline{3} & 0.6\overline{6} \\ 0.3\overline{3} & 0.6\overline{6} \end{pmatrix} \quad (7.5)$$

The final matrix then becomes

$$\mathrm{CPT}_{PT1} = \begin{pmatrix} 0.0 & 0.0 \\ 0.3\overline{3} & 0.6\overline{6} \\ 0.3\overline{3} & 0.6\overline{6} \\ 0.6\overline{6} & 0.3\overline{3} \\ 0.3\overline{3} & 0.6\overline{6} \\ 0.6\overline{6} & 0.3\overline{3} \\ 0.6\overline{6} & 0.3\overline{3} \\ 1.0 & 0.0 \end{pmatrix} \quad (7.6)$$

The CPT of other nodes are also created in the same manner. The complete model with all CPTs is used as a core model to infer the failure probability of each component and failure propagation. It can be noticed that two entries in the first row of the CPT are both 0.0. The probabilities in this row will be updated at runtime, as described in Section 7.4, to reflect the failure probability of that component when other dependent components are healthy.

7.4. Updating the Failure Propagation Model at Runtime

The first row of the CPT indicates the failure probability of the component when other dependent components are functioning correctly. This probability depends on the health of each component and cannot be deduced from the architectural information of the system. Therefore, it must be obtained from another source which are the failure predictors responsible for each component (Chapter 5).

At runtime, a component can exhibit many performance metrics such as response time and resource utilization. A component failure predictor of that component is responsible for predicting if it is going to fail. Since the prediction result of the component failure predictor indicates the probability of a failure occurring in the component itself, this probability then replaces the first row of the CPT of the corresponding component in the model.

For example, assume that the predictor of BT1 predicts that it may fail in 10 minutes with a probability of 0.8. The first row of CPT_{BT3} in Table 7.2b, where DB failure is `False`, will be set to 0.8 and 0.2, accordingly.

The online update process is periodically performed for all component failure predictors. To provide a consistent prediction of the failure propagation, the component failure predictors are set to make predictions with the same lead time, e.g., 10 minutes. This simplifies the inference of the failure propagation discussed in the next section.

Algorithm 7.1 shows the updating process of the FPM. In the first step, an ADM is obtained from the extractor and used to update the structure of the Bayesian network. Then, the component failure probabilities are obtained from the component failure predictors. The first rows of the CPTs of the Bayesian network are updated according to the probabilities. In the last step, the inference of the Bayesian network is carried out to obtain the architecture-aware component failure probabilities.

Algorithm 7.1 Updating Failure Propagation Model

Require: ADM, component failure predictors
1: **while** true **do**
2:     Obtain ADM from the extractor
3:     Update Bayesian network structure
4:     **for all** predictor in component failure predictors **do**
5:         Obtain component failure probabilities
6:         Update CPT of the corresponding component
7:     **end for**
8:     Infer new architecture-aware failure probabilities
9: **end while**

7.5. Inference of the Failure Propagation Model

The inference of the failure propagation is the last step of HORA, which predicts what the effects of component failures can be, i.e., how likely that failures will propagate to other components. Once the component failure probabilities (described in Chapter 5) are updated, Bayesian inference [Bis06] (described in Section 2.2.3) is used to obtain new failure probabilities of all components. This inference takes into account not only their own failure probabilities but also those of their parents and ancestors. If a node's ancestors have high failure probabilities, its failure probability will also be high. Therefore, the inference allows us to model and predict failure propagation from the inside to the outside of the system. At runtime, the inference is done at regular intervals to provide the current failure probabilities of all components.

Let us consider the system in *Running Example 1* (Figure 6.2 on Page 104), which is composed of four types of components, i.e., load balancer (LB), presentation tier (PT), business tier (BT), and data tier (DT). The failure probability of a component in the system can be computed using the joint probability function. For example, the failure probability of BT1 can be written as a joint probability of BT1 and DB since BT1 depends on DB. This probability can be represented as

$$P(\text{BT1}_F = T, \text{DB}_F) = \frac{\sum_{\text{DB}_F \in \{T,F\}} P(\text{BT1}_F = T | \text{DB}_F) P(\text{DB}_F)}{\sum_{\text{BT1}_F, \text{DB}_F \in \{T,F\}} P(\text{BT1}_F | \text{DB}_F) P(\text{DB}_F)} \qquad (7.7)$$

The conditional probabilities and the prior probabilities are computed and obtained from the CPTs of the corresponding components in the FPM as presented in Section 7.3.

In the current state of failure propagation inference, all component failure predictors are configured to provide component failure probabilities based on the same lead time. This simplifies the way the FPM stores the component failure probabilities and allows the existing inference algorithm to be employed. The inference of the FPM is carried out periodically to obtain new failure probabilities in order to reduce the computational complexity. Since the failure probabilities of the components can be obtained at any time, inferring the failure probabilities of all components in the FPM after receiving one data point from a component failure predictor is computationally expensive. Thus, the inference of the FPM is done at regular intervals and can be defined in the Hora's configuration.

It is important to note that there is a trade-off between the quality of the prediction and the computational complexity. If the frequency of the inference is high, i.e., the inference is done immediately after a new data point arrives, the prediction results will represent the true status of the system. However, this results in a high computational complexity since the algorithm has to be executed at the rate that new data points arrive. On the other hand, if the frequency is low, i.e., the algorithm waits until a number of data points arrive or until a certain interval has passed, the prediction results will represent the status of the system in the past. Nevertheless, the algorithm does not have to be executed every often, thus, reducing the computational complexity. Therefore, the frequency of the inference needs to be configured to balance these two aspects.

7.6. Summary

This chapter presents the Failure Propagation Model (FPM) which is the last step of the Hora approach and answers the research question RQ3.1. In this chapter, the FPM is introduced to model the propagation of the failures using the architectural knowledge obtained from the ADM. The transformation from an ADM to an FPM is presented. Moreover, the update process of the FPM at runtime and the inference of the model to obtain architecture-aware component failure probabilities are also presented.

CHAPTER 8

IMPLEMENTATION

This chapter presents two implementations of the HORA approach. Section 8.1 presents the first implementation in Java, which is a proof of concept, aiming at quantitatively evaluating HORA's improvement on the prediction quality over the monolithic approach. Section 8.2 presents the second implementation in Go, which focuses on providing HORA as a tool that can be used for predicting failures in production environments at runtime. The implementations are available in the supplementary material [Pit18].

8.1. Java Implementation

The first implementation of HORA is written in Java. The goal is to prove that the idea of HORA is feasible. Specifically, combining component failure predictors and the architectural knowledge should improve failure prediction of the whole system. This implementation has the following use cases:

- The implementation is executed offline. Specifically, the monitoring data will be first collected from a running system and stored as log files. In addition to the monitoring data, the failures and time of occurrence will also be recorded. These two sources of information are used to train the prediction models.

- The implementation should allow an extensive evaluation of the approach and provide evaluation metrics as results.

Section 8.1.1 describes the overview of the architecture and the components that are involved in the prediction and evaluation processes. Section 8.1.2 describes how the system is instrumented so that the monitoring data can be obtained. Sections 8.1.3 to 8.1.5 present the implementations of the component failure predictors, the Architectural Dependency Model (ADM) and Failure Propagation Model (FPM), respectively.

8.1.1. Architecture Overview

The architecture of this implementation is depicted in Figure 8.1. In this implementation, the HORA approach is split into two phases, which are data collection and evaluation. The data collection focuses on simulating requests from users and collecting the monitoring data from the system. The system is instrumented with Kieker, which is an APM framework (Section 2.3.5.2), to obtain the method response time and resource utilization. The monitoring data is stored in a file which will later be read in the evaluation phase. Furthermore, a SLAstic model, which describes the structure and behavior of the system, is extracted from the data. In addition to the monitoring data, the responses that the users receive are also recorded. This data will indicate whether observable failures have occurred on the client side.

The evaluation, which is the second phase, focuses on creating models that can predict the failures and on evaluating the prediction quality. The implementation is mainly based on Kieker's pipe-and-filter architecture [HWH12]. The monitoring data is read from the file system by Kieker's file system reader. The data is forwarded to the component failure predictors which produce failure probabilities of individual components. The SLAstic model that is created in the data collection phase is transformed to an ADM. The FPM obtains the component failure probabilities and the ADM. Then, it infers new

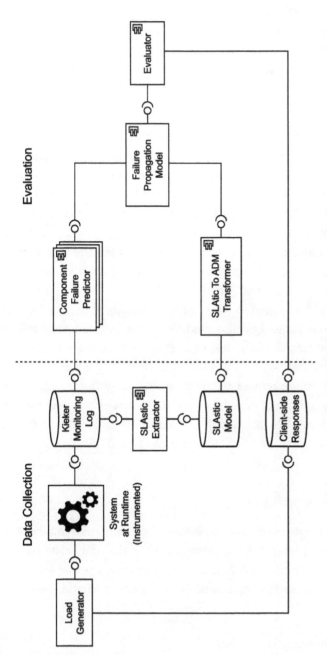

Figure 8.1.: Architecture of Java implementation of HORA

failure probabilities taking into consideration the component dependencies. In the last step, the prediction results are compared to the actual status of the system and the evaluation results are obtained.

8.1.2. System Instrumentation

We employ Kieker to obtain the monitoring data from a running system. The application is instrumented with the code that gets executed before and after each method to trace the call and measure the response time. The code injection functionality is provided by Kieker which employs AspectJ [KHH+01] as the underlying technology to instrument Java applications. However, to monitor remote calls that go across multiple nodes, a new monitoring probe is required to follow the calls throughout the whole distributed system. Two new monitoring probes, i.e., `OperationExecutionJersey-ClientInterceptor` and `OperationExecutionJerseyServerInterceptor` are implemented to intercept the outgoing and incoming calls. The header of each outgoing call is modified to include the trace information, which are the traceID, EOI, and ESS. These variables are extracted by the probe in the remote nodes and used as the traceID for further calls.

In addition to the remote call monitoring, the resource utilization of the nodes needs to be monitored as well. To achieve this, new samplers are implemented using Sigar[1], which is a library to gather system information. These new samplers are `LoadAverageSampler`, `DiskUsageSampler`, and `NetworkUtilizationSampler`.

8.1.3. Component Failure Predictors

This section presents the implementation of component failure predictors. Section 8.1.3.1 presents the implementation of the time series-based failure prediction. Sections 8.1.3.2 and 8.1.3.3 present the implementation of critical event prediction and hard drive failure prediction, which aim at

---

[1]https://github.com/hyperic/sigar

predicting failures based on other types of data and are not built into the core of the HORA implementation.

8.1.3.1. Time Series-based Failure Prediction

The time series-based failure prediction is implemented as filters in Kieker's pipe-and-filter architecture [HWH12]. The filters receive the monitoring data from the reader and predict their values in the future. This data is collected from different sources, e.g., load average and method response time. The corresponding predictors are configured according to the pre-defined configurations, e.g., failure threshold and lead time. The predictors utilize an ARIMA forecaster (Section 2.2.1) implemented in OPAD, which is an online performance anomaly detection plugin for Kieker [Bie12]. OPAD, in turns, employs the package forecast available in R [R C15] for the forecasting algorithms.

8.1.3.2. Critical Event Prediction

The critical event predictors are implemented separately from the main HORA implementation and are not depicted in Figure 8.1. The predictors are implemented as filters in Kieker's pipe-and-filter architecture and are designed for offline evaluation. The log files are first read by a reader filter and forwarded to preprocessing filters to remove redundant information and reduce the size of the logs, as described in Section 5.5.1. The filtered log messages are classified according to the label and used to train the machine learning algorithms that are provided by the Weka library [WFHP16].

8.1.3.3. Hard Drive Failure Prediction

Similar to the critical event predictors, the hard drive failure predictors are implemented separately from the main HORA implementation and are not depicted in Figure 8.1. The hard drive failure predictors are designed for offline evaluation and are implemented in Java. They employ Weka [WFHP16], which is a library for machine learning algorithms. In the first step, the

S.M.A.R.T. data is read from a file and classified based on the time leading to failures. This data is then used in the cross-validation to train the models and to evaluate the prediction quality.

8.1.4. Architectural Dependency Model

The ADM is implemented in Java as a nested HashMap. The first level of the map contains all components in the system as keys. These keys represent the components that require other components. In other words, they are the components that make calls to the others. The values of the first HashMap are another HashMaps. This second map contains called components as keys and the corresponding dependency weights as values.

8.1.5. Failure Propagation Model

The FPM is implemented as a filter in Kieker's pipe-and-filter architecture [HWH12]. The filter has two input ports to obtain the following data:

- The ADM which is extracted from the SLAstic model, and

- The failure probabilities which are produced by the time series-based component failure predictors.

The received ADM is first transformed into an FPM as described in Section 7.3. In the current state, HORA employs the Bayesian network formalism as the underlying technique for the FPM. The Bayesian network library is provided by Jayes, which is a library used in the Code Recommenders project of Eclipse.[1] The Jayes library provides APIs for creating, updating, and inferring the probabilities of random variables of the network.

The received component failure probabilities are updated in the underlying Bayesian network at regular intervals. After each update, the network is solved to obtain new component failure probabilities that take into consideration the dependencies between components in the architectural model.

---

[1] https://github.com/kutschkem/Jayes

8.2. Go Implementation

The second implementation of HORA is written in Go.[1] The goal is to provide an implementation that can make failure predictions in production environments at runtime. This implementation has the following use cases:

- The implementation will be executed online in a containerized environment [Mer14]. The monitoring will be collected from a live system and the failures will be predicted at runtime.

- The implementation should visually present the results of the prediction for all components and the service of the system under test in realtime.

This implementation is a part of the analysis module in the CASPA platform [DHH+17], which is a platform for comparability of architecture-based software performance engineering approaches. The CASPA platform, including the HORA as an analysis module, is publicly available online.[2]

The remainder of this section presents the implementation details. Section 8.2.1 presents the overview of the architecture. Sections 8.2.2 to 8.2.4 present the implementation details of the component failure predictors, the ADM, and the FPM, respectively. The source code of this implementation is publicly available online.[3]

8.2.1. Architecture Overview

The architecture of the Go implementation is depicted in Figure 8.2. Since the goal is to apply HORA in a containerized environment, each component is designed to be deployed as a Docker container.[4] These containers can be deployed in a Kubernetes cluster, which is a container orchestration system.[5]

---

[1]https://golang.org/
[2]https://github.com/spec-rgdevops/CASPA-platform
[3]https://github.com/hora-prediction/hora
[4]https://docker.com/
[5]https://kubernetes.io/

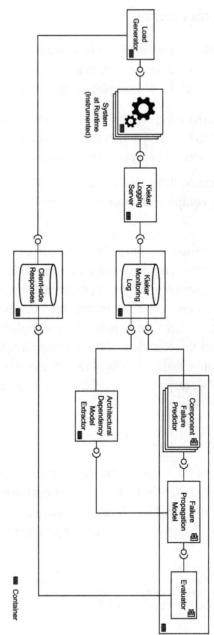

Figure 8.2.: Architecture of Go implementation of HORA

■ Container

In this implementation, the system under test is migrated to Docker containers and instrumented with Kieker. The source code of the migrated application is publicly available online.[1] In contrast to the traditional environment, in which the system under test is deployed on physical servers, Docker uses the libvirt toolkit[2] to run containers in a virtualized environment. This complicates the process of collecting monitoring data since they are not easily accessible from other containers. Therefore, we employ Kieker Logging Server (KLS)[3] to collect monitoring data from all containers and write them to a databases. The database we use in this implementation is InfluxDB,[4] which is a time series database. In addition to the monitoring data, the client-side responses are also stored in an InfluxDB database and will be later used by the evaluator.

For the failure prediction process, the monitoring data is read and split into groups according to components. The corresponding component failure predictors then make predictions and produce failure probabilities. In parallel, an ADM is extracted directly from the same monitoring data, in contrast to the first implementation, which is transformed from a SLAstic model. The ADM extractor in this implementation is split into a separate container that can be deployed and functions independently from the prediction part. This allows the extracted model to be used for other purposes in the future.

In the last step, the component failure prediction results and the ADM are combined in the FPM. New component failure probabilities are computed based on the component dependencies. Finally, the results are compared to the actual status of the system and the evaluation results are generated.

8.2.2. Component Failure Predictors

Similar to the first implementation, the component failure predictors are based on time series forecasting. We utilize an R server [R C15], which is deployed as a container and provides forecasting algorithms. The communi-

---

[1]https://github.com/hora-prediction/recipes-rss-kube
[2]https://libvirt.org/
[3]https://github.com/kieker-monitoring-docker/kieker-logging-server
[4]https://github.com/influxdata/influxdb

cation with the R server is done by preparing the statements that need to be executed and sending them to the server. The results are then returned as text and parsed to obtain the desired values.

8.2.3. Architectural Dependency Model

The ADM extractor in this implementation is re-written to provide realtime extraction based on the monitoring data. The model is extracted directly from the monitoring log collected by Kieker. The extraction is carried out by analyzing the traceID, EOI, and ESS of the traces, as described in Section 2.3.5.2. As depicted in Figure 2.11, this information can be used to discover the call tree of the program. This allows us to extract the component dependencies and the number of times one component calls another.

8.2.4. Failure Propagation Model

The FPM receives component failure probabilities and the extracted ADM through two separate channels, which resemble pipes in the pipe-and-filter architecture. These two pieces of information are continuously sent to the FPM at runtime. The FPM employs `bnlearn`, which is a Bayesian network library available in R [Scu10]. After the model is updated, an inference is carried out in R to obtain new failure probabilities that are aware of the component dependencies.

Figure 8.3 depicts the prediction results of HORA visualized using Grafana,[1] which is a platform for analytics and monitoring. The visualization presents the monitoring data collected from the components in the system, such as method response times, CPU utilization, memory utilization, and network utilization. In addition to the monitoring data, the client-side responses, e.g., end-to-end response time and the HTTP status codes are also presented. Along with the aforementioned monitoring data, the architecture-aware failure probabilities made by HORA are also presented. These include not only the component failure probabilities but also the failure probabilities of the services that the system provides to the end users.

---

[1]https://grafana.com/

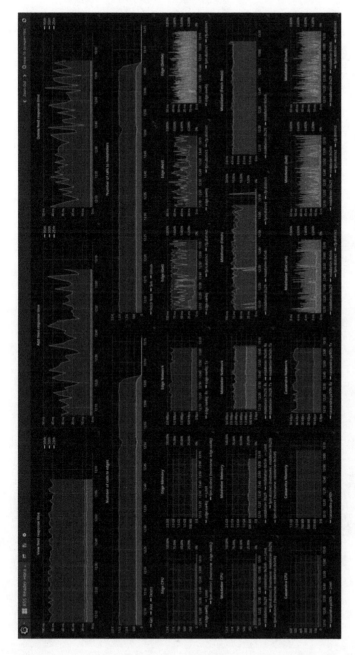

Figure 8.3.: A visualization of the prediction results of HORA at runtime

Part III.

Evaluation

CHAPTER 9

EVALUATION METHODOLOGY

The HORA approach proposed in the previous chapters needs to be evaluated to access whether it can improve the prediction quality of online failure prediction. The evaluation is split into multiple chapters so that each part of the approach can be independently evaluated and optimized for the best results. This chapter provides the overview of the evaluation (Section 9.1), evaluation metrics (Section 9.2) and statistical hypothesis testing (Section 9.3) which is used to evaluate the prediction approaches.

9.1. Overview of Evaluation

The evaluation of the HORA approach is divided into two steps:

- The first step focuses on evaluating the prediction quality of component failure predictors which is split into three chapters:

    - Chapter 10 presents the evaluation of the time series-based failure prediction. The approach introduced in Section 5.4 is evaluated by applying it to Netflix's RSS reader which is a distributed server-side application. The time series data, i.e., CPU utilization and method response time of software components, of the system is monitored and used as symptom to predict upcoming failures.

- Chapter 11 presents the results of the critical event prediction introduced in Section 5.5. The dataset used in the evaluation is event logs that are collected from the Blue Gene/L supercomputer system.

- Chapter 12 presents hard drive failure prediction which is introduced in Section 5.6. The evaluation uses the S.M.A.R.T. data collected from 369 hard drives.

- The second step (Chapter 13) focuses on evaluating the prediction quality of the whole HORA approach. The ADM (Chapter 6) and the results of component failure prediction shall be used to infer the failure propagation probabilities by the FPM. Furthermore, the effects of the ADM on the prediction quality will be investigated.

9.2. Evaluation Metrics

In order to evaluate the prediction quality of different approaches, evaluation metrics are needed to determine whether the result of one approach is better than another. At runtime, a component failure predictor may predict a component to be healthy or to fail in the near future. In the same manner, the actual status of a component at the predicted time can be either healthy or failed. This results in four possible types of outcomes which are as follows [SLM10].

- True positive (TP)—The predictor concludes that a failure is possible and, in the predicted time frame, a failure actually occurs. This is a correct prediction of a failure and we would like to maximize it.

- False positive (FP)—The predictor predicts that a failure will occur but it does not. This is a wrong prediction which we would like to avoid. It can cause unnecessary operations and have high costs to prepare for

Prediction	Actual	
	Failure	**Non-failure**
Failure	True positive (TP)	False positive (FP)
Non-failure	False negative (FN)	True negative (TN)

Table 9.1.: Contingency table

Metric	Formula
Precision	$\dfrac{TP}{TP + FP}$
Recall, True-positive rate (TPR)	$\dfrac{TP}{TP + FN}$
False-positive rate (FPR)	$\dfrac{FP}{FP + TN}$
Accuracy	$\dfrac{TP + TN}{TP + TN + FP + FN}$
F-measure	$\dfrac{2 \cdot \text{Precision} \cdot \text{Recall}}{\text{Precision} + \text{Recall}}$

Table 9.2.: Selected derived evaluation metrics

failure avoidance, e.g., spawning more instances of the services that are predicted to fail.

- False negative (FN)—The predictor predicts that there will be no failure but a failure actually occurs. This type of outcome is also called a *miss* and is also a wrong prediction. If the failure is severe, the consequence can be very catastrophic. For example, a failure of the database that was not predicted can result in a permanent loss of data.

- True negative (TN)—The predictor predicts that there will be no failure and no failure occurs. This is a correct prediction that should also be maximized.

Table 9.1 presents these four basic evaluation metrics as a contingency table. Apart from these basic metrics, more complex metrics can be derived from them and can provide more information regarding the prediction quality. For example, a predictor that always predicts that a component is going to fail will not miss a failure, which results in a high number of TP. However, it will also produce a high number of FP since some of the predicted failures do not occur. Therefore, it is necessary to consider more than one metric when evaluating a prediction approach. The derived metrics that we consider in the evaluation are precision, recall or True-positive rate (TPR), False-positive rate (FPR), accuracy, and F-measure which are listed in Table 9.2. A good predictor would produce a high precision, high recall or TPR, low FPR, and high accuracy. F-measure is a value that represents the harmonic mean of precision and recall [SLM10]. A perfect predictor would have the F-measure value of 1, while the worst prediction would have 0.

Receiver Operating Characteristic (ROC) curves [Faw06] represent the quality of the prediction by relating TPR to FPR for different prediction thresholds, as shown in Figure 9.1. A random predictor that produces alarms at random would achieve a curve that goes from $(0,0)$ to $(1,1)$ (shown as a dotted line). The closer the curve is to the $(0,1)$ point, the better the prediction is. The red dashed line and the blue dotted dashed line present two examples of typical ROC curves. The predictor 1 is better than a random predictor and the predictor 2 is better than the predictor 1. A perfect predictor has a curve that goes from $(0,0)$ to $(0,1)$ and $(1,1)$.

Area under ROC curve (AUC) measures the area that is covered by a ROC curve and allows comparison between different ROC curves. A perfect predictor would have an AUC of 1. The AUC is recommended to be used as a single-number metric for evaluating learning algorithms [Bra97; HL05]. Thus, in our evaluation, the AUC is used as a representative metric for the comparison of the prediction qualities.

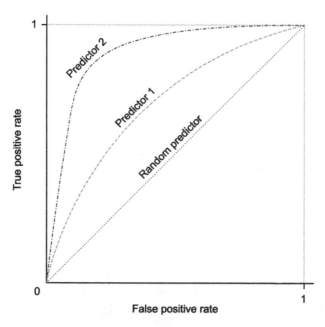

Figure 9.1.: Example of ROC curves

9.3. Statistical Hypothesis Testing

A statistical hypothesis is a statement that describes parameters of populations [MRH09]. An example of a statistical hypothesis is the mean value of the response time of a service. In order to determine if the statistical hypothesis is true, a procedure called *statistical hypothesis testing* is required.

An AUC described in the previous section can be obtained from one run of the evaluation. However, a conclusion of which approach performs better than another based on the data obtained from one run cannot be statistically accepted. This is because there can be many random variables that can influence the results, e.g., one data set may contain signs of failures that are usually not present at runtime and provide advantages to one of the approaches. Thus, comparing the prediction qualities of two prediction approaches requires multiple runs of the experiment which produces a number of the AUCs. In order to make a statistical conclusion, we use two-sided hypothesis testing [WRH+12] to compare the AUC and evaluate the significance of the improvement. The null and alternative hypotheses are defined as follows:

$$H_0 : AUC_{\text{HORA}} = AUC_{Monolithic} \tag{9.1}$$

$$H_1 : AUC_{\text{HORA}} \neq AUC_{Monolithic} \tag{9.2}$$

The result of statistical hypothesis testing is reported as a p-value. The p-value is the probability that the parameter of interest is at least as extreme as the observed value given that the null hypothesis is true [MRH09]. In other words, the smaller the p-value, the more likely that the null hypothesis can be rejected. The method used in testing is introduced by DeLong, DeLong, and Clarke-Pearson [DDC88] to compare two or more AUC. The ROC curves, AUCs, and the results of the evaluation are generated using the pROC package [RTH+11] available in R [R C15].

10

EVALUATION OF TIME
SERIES-BASED FAILURE
PREDICTION

This chapter presents an evaluation of failure prediction using time series-based prediction algorithms. The goal is to predict future observations of time series data, e.g., CPU utilization and service response time. The predictions are then used to estimate the probability of threshold or SLO violations that could result in a service failure.

Section 10.1 presents the research question that will be answered in this chapter. Section 10.2 describes the experiment setup of the evaluation. Section 10.3 presents the results of the experiment. Section 10.4 provides a discussion of the results. Section 10.5 presents the threats to validity of the experiment. Section 10.6 summarizes the evaluation in this chapter.

10.1. Research Question

This chapter focuses on evaluating the prediction quality of the time series-based failure prediction presented in Section 5.4. Furthermore, the evaluation aims to answer the following research question which has been previously stated in detail in Section 4.1:

- RQ1.3: What are the prediction qualities of component failure predictors?

10.2. Experiment Setup

This section presents the details of the experiment setup which are system under test (Section 10.2.1), fault injection (Section 10.2.2), the definition of failures (Section 10.2.3), and the prediction technique (Section 10.2.4).

10.2.1. System Under Test

The distributed RSS feed reader application[1] is originally developed by Netflix to demonstrate their open-source software libraries.[2] The application follows the microservice architectural style which is composed of small autonomous services [New15]. Figure 10.1 shows the web user interface of the application which allows users to view, add, or delete RSS feeds.

The RSS feed reader application is composed of four main components:

- Edge. The edge is a presentation layer that receives requests from users and forwards them to the business layer. Once the business layer completes the business logic, the edge receives the reply, i.e., the RSS feeds, from the business layer and renders the web page that will be viewed by the users.

- Middletier. The middletier is a business layer that receives requests from the presentation layer. The requests may be one of the following

---

[1]https://github.com/Netflix/recipes-rss
[2]https://netflix.github.io/

Figure 10.1.: Web user interface of the RSS feed reader application

types: view feeds, add a feed, or delete a feed. The middletier processes each request according to the type. When a request to view all the feeds is received, the middletier first reads the list of Uniform Resource Locators (URLs) from the database, fetches the feed in Extensible Markup Language (XML) format from each URL, parses them, and returns them to the presentation layer. When a request to add a feed is received, it writes the URL of the feed to the database. When a request to delete a feed is received, it removes the URL of the feed from the database.

- Database. The database is used to store the URL of the feeds. The data in the database can be accessed and modified by the middletier.

- Eureka. Eureka is a service discovery component that is used to register and locate services, i.e., the edges and middletiers. The edges need to communicate with the middletiers in order to fulfill the requests. However, as each component can be scaled horizontally, the list of available components also needs to be kept up-to-date. Eureka also provides load balancing and fail-over. It keeps track of all middletiers and their health by receiving heartbeats from them. If one or more instances of the middletier fail, it will redirect the requests to other running instances.

Figure 10.2 illustrates the architecture of the RSS feed reader application and how the components communicate with each other. In the experiment, two instances of the edge, three instances of the middletier, and one instance of the database are deployed. The database used in this experiment is Apache Cassandra,[1] which is a free and open-source distributed NoSQL database. In addition to the application components that provide the services, two following components are also required:

- Load balancer. A load balancer is a component that is placed between two layers to distribute the workload according to the specified strategies. In this experiment, HAProxy[2] version 1.5.14 is used as an entry point of the application which forwards the requests to three instances of edge service equally.

- RSS feed servers. The goal of the application is to provide a page where users can view, add, and delete feeds. Thus, at least one instance of RSS feed server is required to provide the feeds in XML format. Apache Tomcat,[3] which is a free and open-source Java servlet container, version 8.0.18 is used to host the Rich Site Summary (RSS) feeds.

- Workload generator. To simulate realistic user requests, i.e., view, add, and delete, a workload generator is required. In this experiment, the

---

[1] https://cassandra.apache.org/
[2] http://www.haproxy.org/
[3] http://tomcat.apache.org/

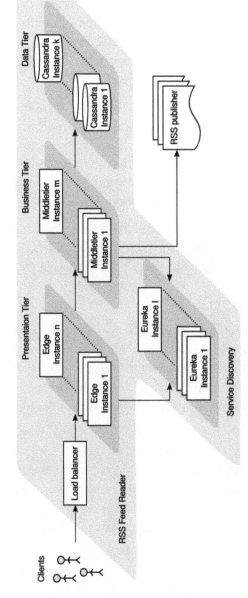

Figure 10.2.: Architecture of RSS feed reader application

workload generator is deployed on a separate node and uses Apache JMeter [Hal08] version 2.9 to generate user requests. The workload generated by each user includes view, add, and delete operations of the RSS feed with an average 3-second think time between two requests. The number of concurrent users is set to 150 throughout the experiment. On average, the workload driver generates approximately 90 requests per second.

The original application by Netflix provides basic functionalities required to demonstrate how their open-source libraries work. However, to support the evaluation of the HORA approach, some modifications and extensions need to be added to the application so that additional information can be obtained. Thus, the following modifications and extensions have been added to the application. The modified application is publicly available online.[1]

- Adding multi-user support. The original application provides multi-user support in the backend of the service, i.e., middletier and database. However, the edge does not provide this functionality. Thus, the frontend has been extended so that it can provide service to multiple users simultaneously.

- Returning error status. When the original application experiences an error, it returns a page indicating that an error has occurred. However, the return code is 200 OK which incorrectly indicates that the request was successful. The return code has been changed to 500 HTTP when an error occurs which helps tracking whether or not the users' requests were successful.

- Upgrading libraries. Some libraries used in the application have been updated to newer versions as the old versions cause intermittent failures when communicating between remote hosts under heavy workload. Jersey,[2] which is a framework for developing RESTful web services, is updated from 1.13 to 1.19. Netty,[3] which is an asynchronous

---

[1]https://github.com/hora-prediction/recipes-rss
[2]https://jersey.github.io/
[3]https://netty.io/

event-driven network application framework, is updated from 3.6.1.Final to 4.0.26.Final.

- Instrumenting application. The application is instrumented using Kieker [HWH12] to monitor application performance. The following performance measures are collected at runtime:
  - Response times of view, add, and delete operations at the system boundary (frontend load balancer),
  - Response times of methods involved in processing requests in all presentation- and business-tier instances,
  - Load average, CPU utilization, memory utilization, and swap utilization of all physical machines.

The described system is deployed on Emulab [HRS+08], which is a large-scale virtualized network testbed. Each of the instances is a physical machine type *pc3000* which is equipped with a 3-GHz 64-bit Xeon processor and 2 GB of physical memory, running Ubuntu 14.04.1 LTS and Java 1.7.0 update 75.

10.2.2. Fault Injection

In our evaluation, we consider three types of faults from real world incidents [PN05a], which are memory leak, system overload, and node crash. We inject one type of these faults into each experiment run. Each run lasts two hours and is repeated 10 times. The reported evaluation metrics are obtained by combining and analyzing the raw prediction results of all runs. The details of each type of faults are described as follows.

Memory Leak—In the experiment, a code is inserted into a function of one of the middletier instances. Every time this function is executed, 1024 bytes of memory will be allocated and never be released. This memory leak occurs for each request that is sent from the presentation tier to this specific instance of the middletier. The workload for this scenario contains 150 users with a ramp-up time of 5 minutes. The experiment runs for 2 hours.

System Overload—System overloads occur when the workload increases, either gradually or abruptly, until the system is not able to handle all the incoming requests. In this scenario, instead of injecting a fault and using a constant workload, we increase the number of users until service failures occur.

Node Crash—Unexpected node crashes are not uncommon in real systems. They can be caused by both software and hardware, such as operating system crashes, hardware failures, or power outages. We introduce this problem by intentionally shutting down two of the business tier instances at 90 and 95 minutes into the experiment. The workload for this scenario is the same as that of the memory leak scenario with 150 users and 5 minute-ramp-up time.

10.2.3. Failure Definition

A service failure is defined as an event that occurs when the service deviates from the correct service [ALRL04]. For example, the deviation of the service can be regarded as an increase in the response time, a service outage, or an incorrect result. In this experiment, we classify a service to be in a healthy or failure state by observing the response time in 2-minute windows. We consider a service to fail if the 95th percentile of the server-side response times of all of the requests in that window exceeds 1 second.

The response time threshold of all methods is set to 1 second in the same manner as the server-side response time. We select this value because it eliminates the need of a training phase while still allowing the component failure predictors to make predictions. An alternative to this is to have the thresholds set manually. However, it is infeasible in practice when the system contains a large number of components. A second alternative is to determine the thresholds by learning the response times of all methods. However, this would introduce a learning phase and the response time could vary depending on the context in which the method would be used.

The failure definition of other architectural entities are set according to the types of the entities. The memory utilization threshold is set to 100% according to its physical limit because after this point, the operating system will start swapping which uses the space on the hard drive. The heap utilization threshold is set to 90%, since the garbage collector is triggered automatically when utilization becomes too high. The load average represents the number of tasks in the CPU queue over time and provides more information than the CPU utilization [Wal06]. For example, a 1-minute load average of 1.0 means that there is one task in the CPU queue on average in the past minute. Since each physical machine used in the experiment is equipped with one CPU (as described in Section 10.2.1), we set the failure threshold of the load average to 1.0.

10.2.4. Prediction Technique

At runtime, the monitoring data, containing execution traces and resource measurements, are aggregated into windows of size 2 minutes, which are then pre-processed according to the type of architectural entity measure. The 95th percentile is calculated for the response time and method response time while the mean is calculated for the load average, memory utilization, and heap utilization.

As mentioned in Chapter 7, we use ARIMA as a component failure predictor. Unless stated otherwise, the configuration parameters of ARIMA are as follows. The size of the historical data for ARIMA is set to 10 minutes. The prediction lead time is 10 minutes with a 95% confidence level.

10.3. Results

In this section, we provide the results and explanation for the experiments with different types of faults.

10.3.1. Memory Leak

The memory leak in one of the business-tier instances causes the memory utilization to increase over time. As shown in Figure 10.3a, at approximately the 52th minute, the component failure predictor for memory in one of the business tier instances predicts that the memory utilization will cross the threshold at the 62th minute with a high probability.

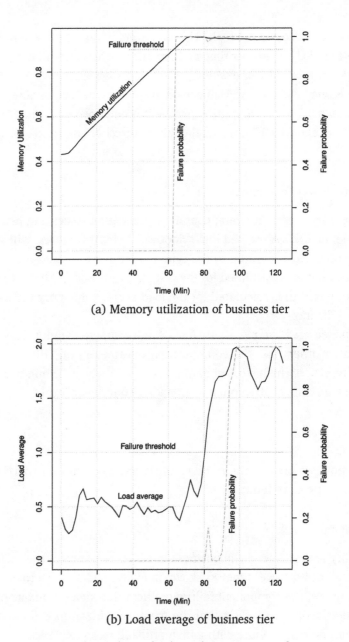

(a) Memory utilization of business tier

(b) Load average of business tier

Figure 10.3.: Timeline plots of selected components for memory leak scenario

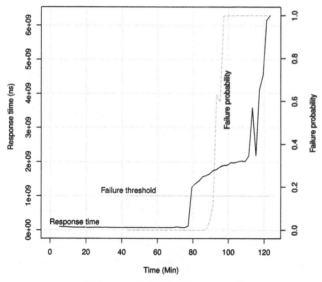

(c) Response time of presentation tier

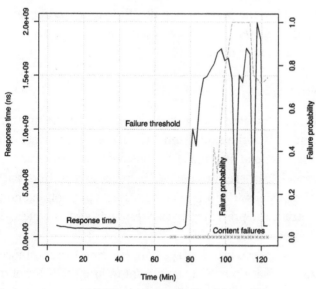

(d) Response time of load balancer

Figure 10.3.: Timeline plots of selected components for memory leak scenario (cont.)

The load average of this business tier instance in Figure 10.3b shows an increase at approximately the same time as when the memory utilization gets close to the threshold. This is due to the garbage collection activity that tries to free up memory. However, this activity is triggered by the memory utilization which is not observable from the load average itself. The component failure predictor for load average does not take this into account and makes predictions based solely on the load average data.

The same effect can be observed for the response time of the presentation tier and the load balancer in Figures 10.3c and 10.3d. Since the memory leak occurs in the business tier, the component predictors of the presentation tier and the load balancer are not aware of the problem and cannot predict it. It is worth noting that, although the presentation tier is closer to the business tier, than the load balancer, the failures in both the presentation tier and load balancer occur at almost the same time. This is due to the fact that the failure propagates from the presentation tier to the load balancer via the remote call. Since each of the calls made to the load balancer results in another remote call to the presentation tier, the failure propagates almost instantly. Thus, the differences in terms of the time of occurrence is minimal and cannot be observed in the figures.

10.3.2. System Overload

The failures caused by overloading the system start occurring at approximately 100 minutes into the experiment. The increasing number of concurrent users causes the load average of the business-tier instances to exceed the failure threshold. As a result, some of the requests sent from the presentation tier to the business tier are rejected. After a pre-defined number of unsuccessful retries, the presentation tier responds with a page indicating that an error has occurred.

Figure 10.4b depicts the load average of one business tier instance which gradually increases over time. The component failure predictor of the load average predicts that there is a small probability, approximately 0.01, that it will reach the threshold. This small probability is due to the fluctuations

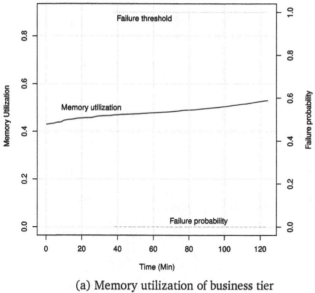

(a) Memory utilization of business tier

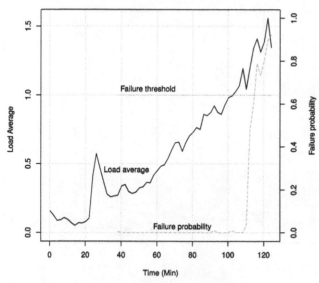

(b) Load average of business tier

Figure 10.4.: Timeline plots of selected components for system overload scenario

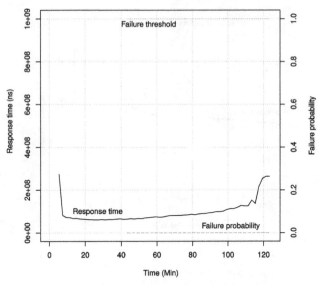

(c) Response time of presentation tier

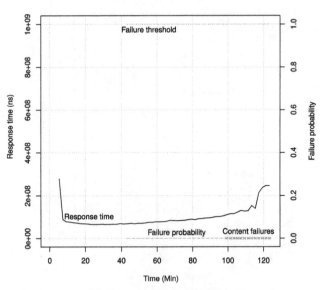

(d) Response time of load balancer

Figure 10.4.: Timeline plots of selected components for system overload scenario (cont.)

of the load average which makes it difficult for ARIMA to accurately make forecasts. Although this small probability can indicate the looming failures, it may also cause a lot of false alarms which results in a high FPR.

The memory utilization, response time of the presentation tier, and the response time of the load balancer remain stable as illustrated in Figures 10.4a, 10.4c and 10.4d. These measures do not exceed the failure threshold and, thus, do not generate any failures.

10.3.3. Node Crash

In this scenario, we intentionally crash the second instance of the business tier at 90 minutes, and the third instance at 95 minutes into the experiment. The one remaining business tier instance has to take over the workload from those that failed.

The crash causes the load average of the remaining instance to increase all of a sudden as can be seen in Figure 10.5b. As a consequence, the response time of the presentation tier and load balancer, shown in Figures 10.5c and 10.5d, also increase unexpectedly. The memory utilization of the remaining instance, as shown in Figure 10.5a, however, remains almost constant similar to that of the system overload scenario.

The component failure predictors of all components are not able to predict this failure because the crash occurs unexpectedly without any preceding symptom.

10.3.4. Overall Prediction Quality

The overall evaluation of the time series component failure predictor is computed by combining the raw results of component failure predictors of all scenarios. A prediction result is a probability of a failure which is annotated with a true label indicating whether a failure actually occurs at the predicted time. The probabilities and labels of all components are combined into one dataset and used to plot a ROC curve. The resulting ROC curve is shown in Figure 10.6d.

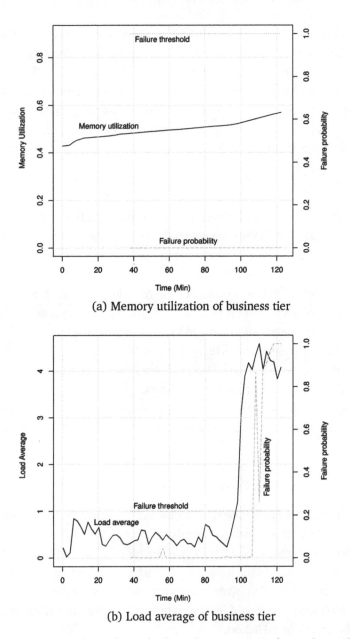

(a) Memory utilization of business tier

(b) Load average of business tier

Figure 10.5.: Timeline plots of selected components for node crash scenario

10 | Evaluation of Time Series-based Failure Prediction

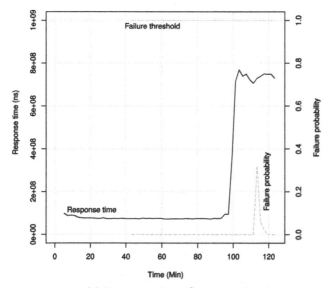

(c) Response time of presentation tier

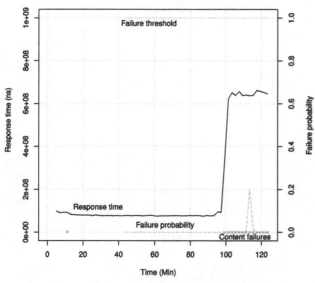

(d) Response time of load balancer

Figure 10.5.: Timeline plots of selected components for node crash scenario (cont.)

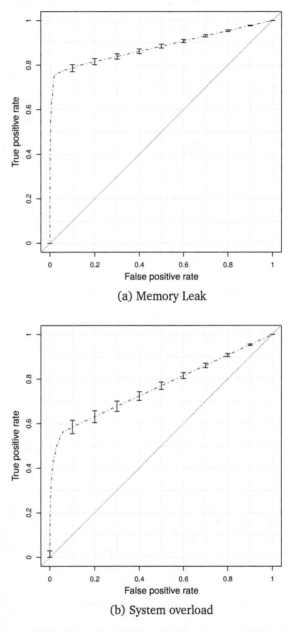

(a) Memory Leak

(b) System overload

Figure 10.6.: ROC curves of ARIMA predictor for different types of faults

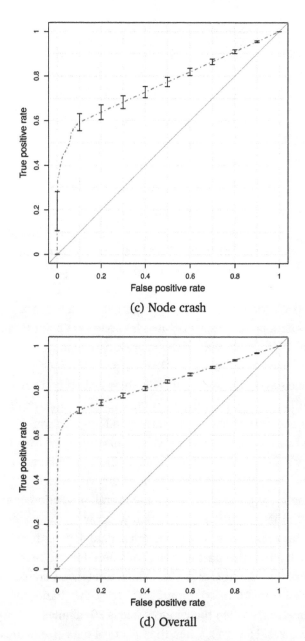

(c) Node crash

(d) Overall

Figure 10.6.: ROC curves of ARIMA predictor for different types of faults
(cont.)

Fault type	Precision	Recall, TPR	FPR	Accuracy	AUC
Memory leak	0.84	0.758	0.024	0.945	0.881
System overload	0.352	0.564	0.059	0.92	0.764
Node crash	0.209	0.582	0.085	0.902	0.766
Overall	0.475	0.692	0.065	0.916	0.837

Table 10.1.: Comparison of all evaluation metrics for the different types of faults

10.3.5. Parameter Impact

ARIMA has various parameters that can be configured and can affect the prediction quality. This section investigates three prediction parameters which are aggregation window size, historical data size, and lead time. The reported metrics are computed by evaluating the raw prediction results of all fault types.

Aggregation Window Size—The aggregation window represents the interval that raw data points are aggregated into one data point for the prediction algorithm. We vary the size of the aggregation window of ARIMA from 2 to 8 minutes. Figure 10.7a shows that the precision increases when the window size increases. The AUC and TPR show a slightly decreasing trend when the size is increased from 2 to 6 minutes but improve significantly when the size becomes 8. This is because small aggregation windows preserve the small variations in the data which causes the predictor to produce a lot of false positives. On the other hand, as the aggregation window gets larger, the small variations in the data are removed which results in the trend becoming more prominent. Thus, the overall prediction quality tends to increase with the size of the aggregation window.

Historical Data Size—The size of historical data denotes how many data points further back in the past ARIMA considers for the prediction. Figure 10.7b shows that the AUC and TPR exhibit a relatively stable trend with the window size from 10 to 40 minutes. On the other hand, the precision and FPR become worse when the window size is 30 minutes but improve for larger window sizes. However, when the historical data size increases to 50

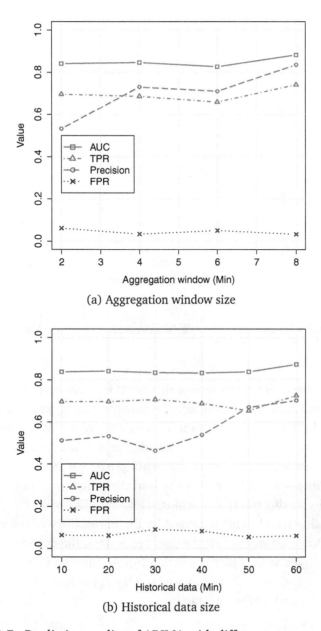

(a) Aggregation window size

(b) Historical data size

Figure 10.7.: Prediction quality of ARIMA with different parameter configurations

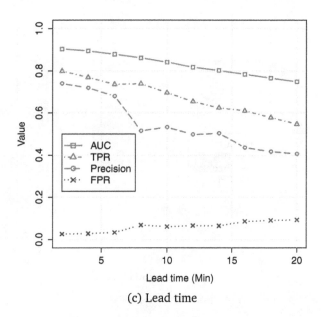

(c) Lead time

Figure 10.7.: Prediction quality of ARIMA with different parameter configurations (cont.)

and 60 minutes, all metrics show a significant improvement. This is because a small historical data window includes only the most recent data points but not those in the past that contain the long term trend. When the window gets larger, those data points are included in the ARIMA for creating the prediction model, which results in a better prediction quality.

Lead Time—When increasing the lead time, the result in Figure 10.7c shows a decreasing trend of precision, TPR, and AUC, while the FPR shows an increasing trend. This is caused by the uncertainty of the prediction. As ARIMA is used to forecast the time series data, the confidence interval becomes larger as we make prediction further into the future. Therefore, choosing an optimal lead time depends on the application and the costs of a false positive and a false negative.

10.4. Discussion

The component failure prediction using ARIMA shows good prediction quality if there are observable symptoms. In the memory leak scenario, the symptom is the increasing memory usage which can be modeled and predicted by ARIMA. On the other hand, if the symptom does not exhibit an obvious trend, as in the system overload scenario, ARIMA may not be able to model and predict future observations with acceptable prediction quality. Furthermore, if the error does not generate any symptom, i.e., in the case of a node crash, the failure cannot be predicted.

10.5. Threats to Validity

We inject faults that trigger application failures in our experiments, which is a common practice in assessing dependability [IV14; NCM16], e.g., fault tolerance or failure prediction. It is possible that the failures that occur at runtime may be caused by other hidden problems rather than those that we inject. In our evaluation, the failures that occur in the memory leak scenario can be caused by a system overload if the workload is too high. As a result, an attempt to predict failures caused by a memory leak will also predict failures of the system overload problem. Therefore, the workload has to be chosen carefully. If the workload is too high, it may cause system overload while other types of faults are injected. If the workload is too low, it may take a lot longer until an injected fault causes a failure.

Each data point of the time series data is obtained by aggregating raw data in a time window. Different aggregation methods, e.g., mean, median, percentile, are used to obtain the aggregated data. It is possible that the numbers of raw data points in the windows are not equal, i.e., some windows may contain more data points than the others depending on the workload. In this experiment, we assume that the number of data points in each window is sufficiently high so that the aggregated data can be accurately computed.

To systematically evaluate our approach, a controlled environment is needed, which includes a usage profile and the types of failures. We conduct a lab study with fault injection which presents two main threats to external validity. First, we consider only one system. Therefore, we select an open-source application that is representative for the state-of-the-art enterprise systems, in terms of architectural style (microservice-based [New15]) and technology (NetflixOSS ecosystem[1]). Second, our experiment did not cover all possible types of faults. Since covering all possible fault types is practically infeasible, we select three representative fault types from real world incidents based on Pertet and Narasimhan [PN05a]. The possibility to reduce these threats for future studies would be that the community makes suitable data available and develops a benchmark for online failure prediction techniques.

10.6. Summary

This chapter presents the evaluation of the time series-based failure prediction and answers research question RQ1.3. The results show that the time series-based failure predictor using ARIMA can predict the failures caused by memory leak. For system overload, the predictor can predict the failures with small probabilities which may result in a high FPR. In the node crash scenario, the predictor is not able to predict the failures since there is no symptom that precedes the failure. Lastly, different configurations of the ARIMA are evaluated. The results show that the configurations, which are aggregation window size, historical data size, and lead time, can have significant impact on the prediction quality. Nevertheless, these parameters have to be chosen depending on the application.

---

[1] https://netflix.github.io/

11

EVALUATION OF CRITICAL EVENT PREDICTION

The previous chapter presents the prediction techniques that can be used to predict failures for time series data. This chapter extends the scope of the prediction by applying them to predict failures based on event logs in supercomputers. The goal is to 1) classify events into categories based on the similarity of the event patterns, and 2) predict critical events in the near future based on the past events. The results presented in this chapter are the classification and prediction quality of two different algorithms, namely, naïve Bayes and C4.5.

Section 11.1 presents the research question that will be answered in this chapter. Section 11.2 describes the experiment setup of the evaluation. Section 11.3 presents the results of the experiment. Section 11.4 presents the threats to validity of the experiment. Section 11.5 summarizes the evaluation in this chapter.

11.1. Research Question

This chapter focuses on evaluating the prediction quality of the critical event prediction presented in Section 5.5. Furthermore, the evaluation aims to answer the following research question which has been previously stated in detail in Section 4.1:

- RQ1.3: What are the prediction qualities of component failure predictors?

11.2. Experiment Setup

This section provides details of the system under test, dataset, and the prediction techniques used in the evaluation.

11.2.1. System Under Test

The system under test in this evaluation is Blue Gene/L. Blue Gene/L is a supercomputer created by IBM and the Lawrence Livermore National Laboratory to achieve the goal of a high performance at a low price and power consumption [AAA+02]. It is a parallel system composed of 65,536 compute nodes based on a new architecture that uses system-on-a-chip technology. Each node is equipped with IBM PowerPC embedded CMOS processors and DRAM which allows 1024 compute nodes to be placed within one rack. The machine has a total of 131,072 processors and 32,768 GB of RAM, providing processing power of 360 teraFLOPS and was operational from 2004 to 2007.

11.2.2. Dataset

The dataset used in the evaluation is a log file which contains 215 days of log messages generated by a Blue Gene/L supercomputer [OS07]. Each message contains the category (label), the timestamp (GMT), the date, the name of the device, and the actual message. The category or label of each message is identified and added by the system administrator. It indicates the type of the alert that the respective message represents. As presented in Table 5.1 (Page 93), there are 42 types of labels in total, including the empty label.

The log file of Blue Gene/L contains a large number of log messages and all of the data cannot be processed at once in the evaluation. We, thus, split the log file into blocks where each block contains approximately the same number of log messages. However, the log messages are not generated uniformly over time, i.e., some types of messages may occur more often at the beginning of the file and vice versa. If the blocks are split by the temporal ordering of the messages, the non-uniform distribution can affect the evaluation since some types of messages may not occur in some blocks. Therefore, we used stratified sampling to maintain the proportion of the types of messages in all blocks. Stratification is the process of splitting data into subgroups, called strata [HSM01]. The strata are homogeneous, which means that each group, or stratum, contains the same proportions of the labels. For example, assuming one label accounts for 15% of the whole dataset. The number of messages with that label in each stratum will also be 15%. The stratification is carried out by analyzing the distribution of the message types and distributing them across the strata while keeping the same distribution in each stratum. This ensures that the data still maintains the same characteristics even though it is split into smaller groups.

11.2.3. Prediction Technique

The machine learning techniques used to predict critical events are naïve Bayes, which is a probabilistic model, and C4.5, which is a decision tree-based algorithm (Section 2.2.2). The machine learning library used in our evaluation is Weka [WFHP16]. In order to determine the classification quality, we use the common approach of 10-fold cross-validation which splits the data of each block into 10 parts and uses 9 parts for training the model and 1 part for the validation. The validation is repeated 10 times and the final result is obtained by averaging the results of all runs. We used the standard metrics as described in Section 9.2 to evaluate the experiment results.

11.3. Results

This section presents the results of critical event prediction. The section is divided into three parts. Section 11.3.1 presents the results of system event classification. Section 11.3.2 presents the impact of the preprocessing of the log messages. Section 11.3.3 presents the results of system event prediction.

11.3.1. Quality of System Event Classification

For event classification, we selected two attributes of the log messages and used them to train the models. These attributes are the label and the actual message of the log. The other attributes, such as timestamp and location, are neglected as they are independent and do not contribute to the assignment of the label of the message.

Figure 11.1 illustrates the precision and recall of classifying the label KERNMNTF over 19 blocks. The log file is split into blocks using stratified sampling and normalized according to Section 5.5.1.1. It can be seen from both plots that precision and recall are similar in all blocks. This result concludes that the log file can be split and evaluated separately without significant deviation between blocks. In terms of computational complexity, since the log normalization is a rule-based algorithm, its computational complexity is very low and is not considered in this experiment.

Figure 11.2 illustrates the F-measure of three configurations of event classification, namely *(i.)* naïve Bayes without normalization, *(ii.)* naïve Bayes with normalization, and *(iii.)* C4.5 with normalization. Figure 11.2a is the result of applying naïve Bayes on the original unfiltered log messages. As the log file is not normalized, the messages contain noise from the numerical values, weak words, etc. This noise results in the highly varying F-measure across different labels. Figures 11.2b and 11.2c illustrate the F-measure of classification using naïve Bayes and C4.5 on the normalized log file. The results show significant improvements of all labels over the original log file. Furthermore, on average, C4.5 performs better than naïve Bayes. Specifically, the number of labels for which naïve Bayes has a recall of zero—leading to

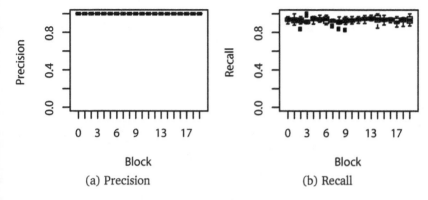

(a) Precision   (b) Recall

Figure 11.1.: Precision and recall of KERNMNTF label using naïve Bayes on normalized log file

an undefined F-measure—is considerably higher than for C4.5.

From the classification results, we can conclude that log normalization helps increase the classification quality as the noise in the messages is filtered out. Moreover, C4.5 outperforms naïve Bayes with F-measure values of 1 for classifying most of the labels.

11.3.2. Impact of Log Filtering

Figure 11.3 shows the number of log messages with INFO severity plotted according to their temporal position in the log file. By comparing the y-axis of the plots in Figures 11.3a and 11.3b, it can be observed that there is a significant reduction in the number of peaks of similarly labeled records located close to each other. While there are more than 130,000 log records with INFO severity during the $2,932$th hour, after filtering there remain only less than 30 for ASF and 400 for tuned ASF and DRF, as depicted in Figures 11.3c and 11.3d. This shows that the filters are capable of effectively eliminating large amounts of redundant log records that occur close to each other.

To evaluate the impact of the log filtering on the event classification, the ASF and DRF techniques (see Section 5.5.1.2) are applied to the log

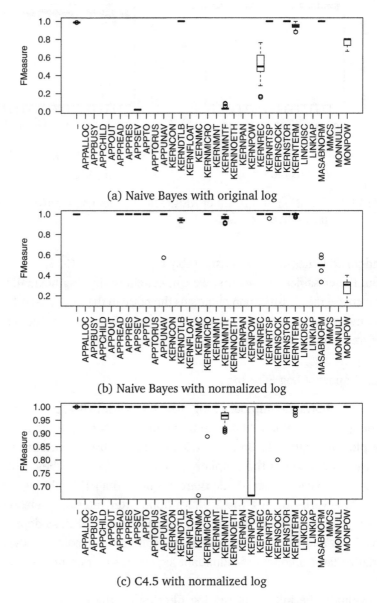

(a) Naive Bayes with original log

(b) Naive Bayes with normalized log

(c) C4.5 with normalized log

Figure 11.2.: F-measure of event classification using different algorithms

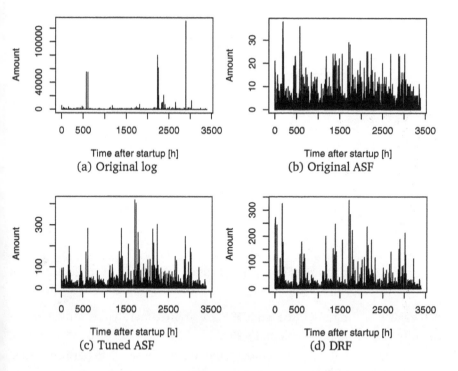

Figure 11.3.: Number of messages with INFO severity before and after applying different filters

messages to produce a reduced set of log records. The log messages that are the output of the filters are used as a training set for the machine learning algorithms. Once the algorithms are trained, the classification is done on the original set of log messages excluding those that are used in the training. It is important to note that—as the log file is large—the log messages are split into blocks where each block contains 500,000 log messages and the evaluation is carried out for every block.

The impact of the filtering on the system event classification is depicted in Figure 11.4. The first and the second boxes show the F-measure of the original ASF and the ASF that is tuned to produce the best result. The third box shows the F-measure when applying DRF. It can be seen that the

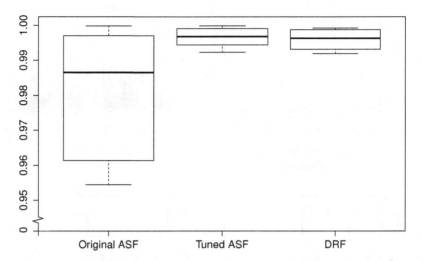

Figure 11.4.: F-measure of event classification when applying different filters

F-measure of the tuned ASF and DRF are approximately the same but are slightly higher than the original ASF.

This result concludes that, although the tuned ASF and DRF perform better than the original ASF, the improvement is not quite significant. Moreover, the tuned ASF is specifically adjusted for this set of data and may not produce as good results for log files collected from other systems. Nonetheless, the DRF which we developed proves to be as effective as the tuned ASF in filtering out the redundant log messages with less computational complexity.

11.3.3. Quality of System Event Prediction

The system event prediction described in Section 5.5.3 has a number of parameters, i.e., number of past observations, lead time, prediction window, and sensitivity. These parameters are evaluated individually by varying the value of one parameter while fixing the others. We experimented with various machine learning algorithms, e.g., naïve Bayes, C4.5, Random Forest, RepTree, K-Star, K-nearest neighbours on the normalized log messages and filtered by DRF. The preliminary results show that the naïve Bayes and C4.5

Algorithm	Number of past observations						
	1	2	3	4	6	8	16
NaiveBayes	**0.603**	0.517	0.506	0.500	0.501	0.501	0.503
C4.5	0.621	0.626	0.624	0.624	0.624	0.626	**0.634**

(a) Different numbers of past observations

Algorithm	Lead time (sec)						
	0	60	120	300	600	1200	2800
NaiveBayes	**0.663**	0.589	0.547	0.517	0.506	0.511	0.506
C4.5	**0.877**	0.672	0.634	0.627	0.624	0.640	0.625

(b) Different lead time

Algorithm	Prediction window (sec)						
	60	120	300	600	1200	2800	4800
NaiveBayes	0.491	0.493	0.485	0.506	0.511	0.532	**0.553**
C4.5	0.579	0.578	0.598	0.624	0.640	0.625	**0.635**

(c) Different prediction window

Algorithm	Sensitivity						
	1%	5%	10%	20%	40%	80%	100%
NaiveBayes	**0.546**	0.522	0.516	0.506	0.462	0.519	0.399
C4.5	0.523	0.572	0.609	0.624	**0.691**	0.234	-

(d) Different sensitivity

Table 11.1.: F-measures of system event prediction with different parameter configurations

outperform the others. Hence, the following results are the experiment of naïve Bayes and C4.5 as the exhaustive experiment of all algorithms with all configurations is computationally expensive and infeasible.

Table 11.1a shows the resulting F-measures for predicting the future event when the number of past observations is varied from 1 to 16. For this configuration, the lead time and the length of the prediction window are set to 600 seconds, and the sensitivity is set to 20%. From the table, naïve Bayes appears to have the highest F-measure when taking into account only one past observation while C4.5 has the highest F-measure with 16 past observations.

Table 11.1b presents the resulting F-measures when the lead time varies from 0 to 2,800 seconds with 3 past observations, a prediction window of 600 seconds, and sensitivity at 20%. From the table, we can observe that the lead time of 0 seconds has the best F-measure. In other words, our prediction is most accurate when the prediction window starts right after the observation window.

Table 11.1c shows the resulting F-measures for prediction windows from 60 to 4,800 seconds with 3 past observations, a lead time of 600 seconds, and sensitivity at 20%. It is obvious that the longer the prediction window, the better the F-measure. This is because a longer prediction window covers a longer time span which increases the chance of including more events in that period. However, there is a trade-off between prediction accuracy and the significance of the prediction since the longer the prediction window is, the less useful it becomes. In other words, it does not provide much information to the system operators if the system is predicted to fail during the next months or years. Therefore, the selection of the prediction window is context-dependent and needs to be configured according to the target system.

The last parameter of the prediction is the sensitivity. The result is shown in Table 11.1d. The best sensitivity for naïve Bayes is 1% while C4.5 performs best with 40%. It is worth noting that, the higher the sensitivity, the lower the F-measure. The reason is because higher sensitivity means more log messages have to have labels other than "-". This is especially difficult if the sensitivity is 100% which means there can be no "-" label in the prediction window.

In conclusion, the parameters that result in a similar effect for both algorithms are the lead time and the length of the prediction window. The smaller the lead time, the better the accuracy. This is because it is easier and more accurate to make predictions in the near future than further away in time. Likewise, the longer the prediction window, the better the accuracy because it increases the chance of having the predicted events occurring in that time span.

On the other hand, the number of past observations and the sensitivity show opposite effects on the two algorithms. While the higher number of past observations reduces the accuracy of naïve Bayes, it increases the accuracy of C4.5. However, in this case, the effect of the sensitivity does not seem to be correlated with the prediction accuracy and, therefore, should be adjusted specifically per application.

11.4. Threats to Validity

The evaluation of critical event prediction in this chapter is carried out based on the event logs obtained from the Blue Gene/L supercomputer. This poses a threat to external validity as the data is collected from one system. Furthermore, the preprocessing, log message normalization, and log message filtering are designed and optimized to produce the best results based on this dataset. The event logs collected from other system may have different characteristics that require re-tuning of these processes.

The algorithms that we used in the evaluation are implemented and provided by the Weka library [WFHP16]. There may be other algorithms that perform better than these selected ones but are not available in the Weka library. Therefore, we obtained preliminary results from the available algorithms and selected the algorithms that produce the best results, which are naïve Bayes and C4.5.

11.5. Summary

This chapter presents the evaluation of the critical event prediction and answers research question RQ1.3. The event classification results show that the C4.5 algorithm produces F-measure of 1 in most cases and outperforms the naïve Bayes algorithm. The results of event log filtering shows that the DRF performs as well as the ASF in removing redundancy in the logs with less complexity. Lastly, the results of event prediction show that critical events can be predicted by analyzing the past events. The results also shows that the C4.5 algorithm slightly outperforms the naïve Bayes algorithm in most cases. However, in practice, the configuration of the predictors need to be set based on the requirements and can be different according to the application.

11 | Evaluation of Critical Event Prediction

12

EVALUATION OF HARD DRIVE FAILURE PREDICTION

This chapter presents the evaluation of hard drive failure prediction techniques. The goal of this chapter is to compare the prediction quality of different machine learning techniques to predict failures in hard drives. The evaluation results are presented and a discussion is provided regarding which predictors should be used for different scenarios.

Section 12.1 presents the research question that will be answered in this chapter. Section 12.2 describes the experiment setup of the evaluation. Section 12.3 presents the results of the experiment. Section 12.4 provides a discussion of the results. Section 12.5 presents the threats to validity of the experiment. Section 12.6 summarizes the evaluation in this chapter.

12.1. Research Question

This chapter focuses on evaluating the prediction quality of the hard drive failure prediction presented in Section 5.6. Furthermore, the evaluation aims to answer the following research question which has been previously stated in detail in Section 4.1:

- RQ1.3: What are the prediction qualities of component failure predictors?

In addition to the prediction quality, the time required for training the machine learning algorithms and the time required for making predictions will also be investigated.

12.2. Experiment Setup

This section provides details of the dataset, the failure definition, and the prediction technique used in the evaluation.

12.2.1. Dataset

The S.M.A.R.T. dataset used to evaluate hard drive failure prediction is taken from 369 drives, 178 of which are good drives and 191 of which have failed during operation. This dataset has originally been used by Murray, Hughes, and Kreutz-Delgado [MHK05] and has been made publicly available by the authors. The total number of recorded parameters in this dataset is 64, including the class value which indicates whether the drive eventually failed. The whole dataset contains 68,411 instances. Similar to [MHK05], we select 26 indicative parameters for our experiment, which are hours before failure, GList1–3, PList, Servo1–3, Servo5, Servo7–8, Servo10, ReadError1–3, ReadError18–20, and FlyHeight5–12. The excluded parameters are drive serial numbers, hours of operation, and other parameters whose values are constant throughout the monitoring period.

12.2.2. Failure Definition

Before the learning algorithms are applied, the instances in the training set that represent failing and non-failing drives have to be separated so that they can be used to train different prediction models. However, if only the instances that were collected at the time of failures are used to train the failing model, this model will not be able to make predictions as it can recognize only the instances when the drives fail, not before they fail. Therefore, the instances that are collected before the failures should also be used to train the failing model. To determine how long this period should be, let us make two assumptions. First, we assume that the drive exhibits different characteristics throughout its life time. The prediction model that is trained with the instances collected from any operation period will be able to recognize them at runtime. Second, we assume that a sufficient warning time should be seven days before a drive fails. This will give system administrators enough time to prepare for the failure. As a result, the instances that were collected within seven days before the failures are used to train the failing model, while those that are collected before seven days are used to train the non-failing model.

12.2.3. Prediction Technique

We applied 21 machine learning algorithms in six categories, as described in Section 2.2.2, which are:

- *Probabilistic models:* Naïve Bayes Classifier (NBC), Multinomial Naïve Bayes Classifier (MNBC), and Bayesian Network (BN)

- *Decision trees:* C4.5, Reduced Error Pruning Tree (REPTree), and Random Forest (RF)

- *Rule-based algorithms:* ZeroR, OneR, Decision Table (DT), Repeated Incremental Pruning to Produce Error Reduction (RIPPER), and PART

- *Hyperplane separation:* Support Vector Machine (SVM), Sequential Minimal Optimization (SMO), and Stochastic Gradient Descent (SGD)

- *Function approximation:* Simple Logistic Regression (SLR), Logistic Regression (LR), Multilayer Perceptron (MP), and Voted Perceptron (VP)

- *Instance-based learning:* Nearest Neighbor Classifier (NNC), K-Star, and Locally Weighted Learning (LWL)

These algorithms, which are implemented in Weka [WFHP16] version 3.7.5, are applied to the preprocessed dataset and evaluated for the prediction quality of each technique in terms of the evaluation metrics described in Section 9.2. The evaluation is carried out on a physical computer equipped with a quad-core Intel Xeon E31220 processor running at 3.10 GHz with 16 GB of RAM and with Ubuntu Server 12.04.2 LTS as operating system. We used Java version 1.7.0 (Java Virtual Machine (JVM) v. 21.0-b17; Java Runtime Environment (JRE) v. 1.7.0-b147). The initial and maximum amount of heap space available for the JVM are both set to 4 GB in each of the experiments. No other tasks were executed on the machine during the experiment run.

The configurations of the algorithms in the experiment are set to the default values, as the main focus of this work is to compare the prediction qualities between algorithms. The exhaustive parameter tuning of all algorithms is computationally expensive and almost infeasible.

12.3. Results

The experiment in this section is divided into two parts. The first part is the comparison of the prediction quality of each algorithm based on the same dataset. The second part is the comparison of the time needed for the algorithms to build prediction models during the training phase and making prediction at runtime.

12.3.1. Prediction Quality

To measure the prediction quality (in terms of the metrics described in Section 9.2), each algorithm is trained with the instances in the dataset. The trained algorithms are used to make predictions. The results are the average values over 10-fold cross-validation.

Figure 12.1 illustrates the ROC curves of the 21 algorithms. In the very high quality region, the algorithms that have approximately the same level of prediction quality are NNC, RF, C4.5, REPTree, RIPPER, PART, and K-Star. Among the best algorithms, the one that has the highest TPR with low FPR is NNC. However, when the FPR increases, NNC is outperformed by RF. On the other hand, the algorithms that perform poorly are SLR, SGD, SMO, SVM, and ZeroR, showing a prediction quality close to a random predictor.

The algorithms that exhibit only one or two points in the curve are the ones that do not produce class probability but rather give out the predicted class (failure or non-failure) as output. In other words, the threshold that separates failing and non-failing instances is fixed and cannot be varied to adjust the trade-off between TPR and FPR. Thus, these algorithms result in straight lines that go diagonally from (0,0) to (1,1) in the plot. These algorithms are NNC, K-Star, OneR, ZeroR, SGD, SMO, MNBC, and SVM.

Table 12.1 summarizes the prediction quality of all machine learning algorithms. The decision threshold for all classifiers is set to the point with the maximum F-measure. This algorithm configuration is used to obtain the values of the evaluation metrics.

By using the F-measure as the primary metric, the best algorithm appears to be the NNC with F-measure 0.976, followed by RF and C4.5 at 0.957 and 0.946, respectively. Nevertheless, the algorithms in the upper half of the table have F-measure values higher than 0.6, while four algorithms in the lower half score lower than 0.1. For the highest TPR, recall, accuracy, and F-measure, NNC outperforms all other algorithms. On the other hand, for the highest precision, SVM performs best, followed by NNC. However, if a low FPR is the most important metric, for example, when the cost of a false alarm is very high, SMO, and SVM might be the best choices as they can achieve the lowest possible FPR, namely 0, although the other metrics are not very high.

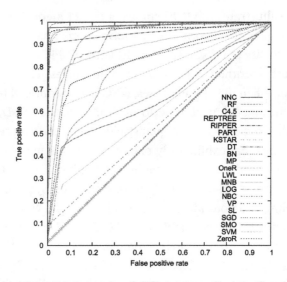

Figure 12.1.: ROC curves of different prediction algorithms

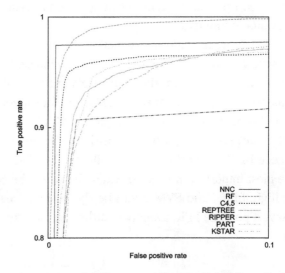

Figure 12.2.: ROC curves of different prediction algorithms (excerpt from Figure 12.1)

12 | Evaluation of Hard Drive Failure Prediction

Algorithm	TPR	FPR	Precision	Recall	Accuracy	F-Measure	AUC
NNC	**0.974**	0.003	0.977	**0.974**	**0.993**	**0.976**	0.986
RF	0.943	0.004	0.971	0.943	0.989	0.957	**0.998**
C4.5	0.942	0.008	0.95	0.942	0.986	0.946	0.973
REPTree	0.913	0.012	0.921	0.913	0.978	0.917	0.982
RIPPER	0.907	0.013	0.915	0.907	0.976	0.911	0.954
PART	0.89	0.012	0.921	0.89	0.975	0.906	0.975
K-Star	0.875	0.012	0.921	0.875	0.973	0.898	0.981
DT	0.668	0.028	0.785	0.668	0.931	0.722	0.936
BN	0.735	0.078	0.592	0.735	0.897	0.656	0.934
MP	0.585	0.032	0.739	0.585	0.917	0.653	0.89
OneR	0.624	0.06	0.616	0.624	0.897	0.62	0.782
LWL	0.652	0.082	0.552	0.652	0.883	0.598	0.833
MNBC	0.252	0.061	0.388	0.252	0.846	0.305	0.603
LR	0.124	0.012	0.618	0.124	0.872	0.206	0.697
NBC	0.118	0.022	0.457	0.118	0.863	0.188	0.789
VP	0.094	0.013	0.527	0.094	0.867	0.16	0.544
SLR	0.08	0.008	0.598	0.08	0.87	0.14	0.665
SGD	0.022	0.001	0.792	0.022	0.868	0.044	0.511
SMO	0.015	0	0.86	0.015	0.868	0.029	0.507
SVM	0.007	0	**0.984**	0.007	0.867	0.014	0.503
ZeroR	0	0	0	0	0.866	0	0.5

Table 12.1.: Prediction quality of the selected algorithms ordered by F-measure

12.3.2. Training and Prediction Time

The measurement of training and prediction time of the algorithms is done by measuring the time the algorithms take to train and make predictions for 68,411 instances of data. This large number of instances is used so as to emphasize the difference between slow and fast algorithms, as shown in Figure 12.3. The results are the average of the training and prediction time across 100 runs, except for the results of LWL, K-Star, and SVM. Their results are the average across 10 runs since these algorithms require a very long training or prediction time.

Table 12.2 provides further time statistics for each algorithm. As can be seen, the fastest algorithms in terms of training time are those in the category of instance-based learning and simple classifiers, i.e., LWL, K-Star, and NNC, which take less than 0.01 seconds to train the model using 68,411 instances. The highest training time is required by SVM, which takes approximately 33 minutes, followed by SLR and MP at approximately four and three minutes,

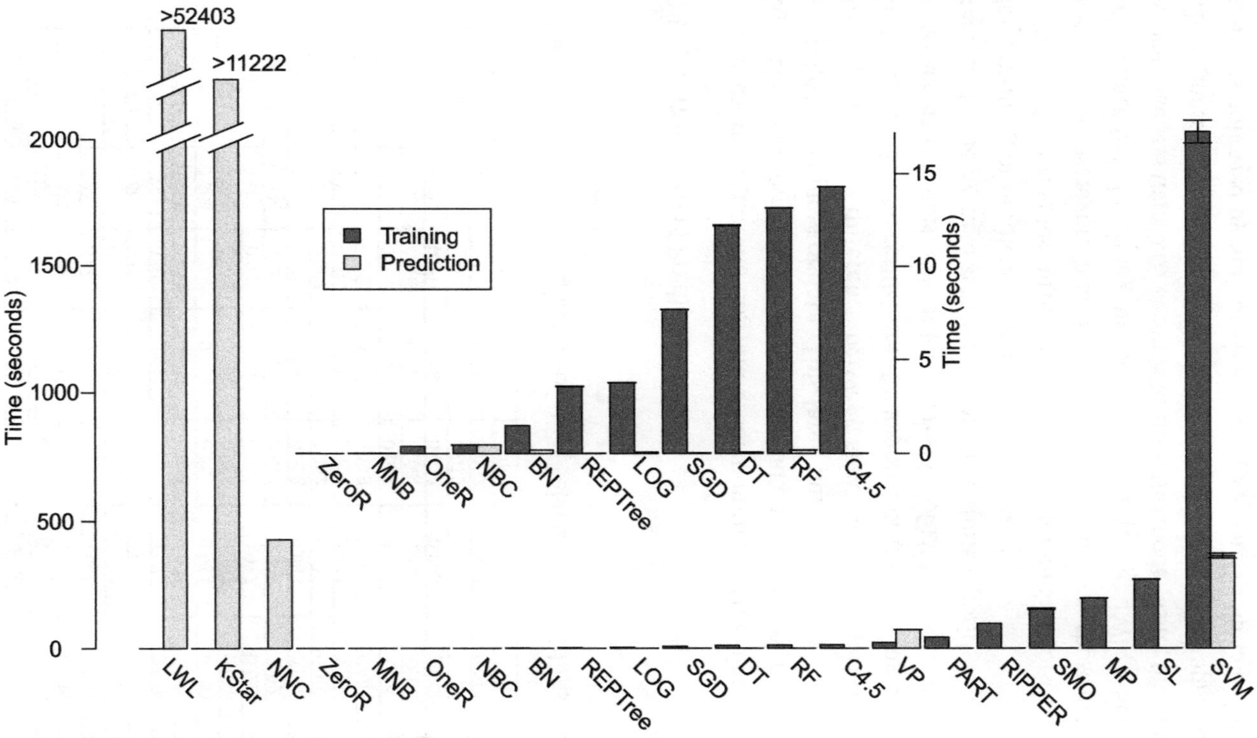

Figure 12.3.: Mean training and prediction time of the selected algorithms. The inner barplot is an enlarged version of the times for selected algorithms.

12 | Evaluation of Hard Drive Failure Prediction

Algorithm	Training (seconds)					Prediction (seconds)				
	Mean	(95% CI)	Q_1	Q_2	Q_3	Mean	(95% CI)	Q_1	Q_2	Q_3
LWL*	0.01	(±<0.01)	0.01	0.01	0.01	52403.33	(±3907.99)	48588.27	49598.24	54346.42
K-Star*	0.01	(±<0.01)	0.01	0.01	0.01	11446.98	(±177.08)	11222.57	11367.73	11707.61
NNC	0.01	(±<0.01)	0.01	0.01	0.01	428.64	(±0.16)	428.01	428.42	429.10
ZeroR	0.01	(±<0.01)	0.01	0.01	0.01	<0.01	(±<0.01)	<0.01	<0.01	<0.01
MNBC	0.02	(±<0.01)	0.01	0.01	0.01	0.01	(±<0.01)	0.01	0.01	0.01
OneR	0.38	(±<0.01)	0.37	0.37	0.38	<0.01	(±<0.01)	<0.01	<0.01	<0.01
NBC	0.45	(±0.01)	0.45	0.45	0.46	0.46	(±<0.01)	0.46	0.46	0.46
BN	1.48	(±<0.01)	1.46	1.47	1.49	0.19	(±<0.01)	0.18	0.19	0.19
REPTree	3.56	(±0.02)	3.53	3.56	3.60	0.01	(±<0.01)	0.01	0.01	0.01
LR	3.76	(±0.01)	3.71	3.73	3.80	0.06	(±<0.01)	0.06	0.06	0.06
SGD	7.68	(±0.01)	7.66	7.68	7.70	0.04	(±<0.01)	0.03	0.04	0.04
DT	12.20	(±0.02)	12.11	12.21	12.28	0.06	(±<0.01)	0.06	0.06	0.06
RF	13.14	(±0.01)	13.12	13.14	13.16	0.18	(±0.01)	0.16	0.20	0.20
C4.5	14.28	(±0.01)	14.24	14.27	14.32	0.02	(±<0.01)	0.02	0.02	0.02
VP	22.48	(±0.06)	22.33	22.46	22.66	73.80	(±0.51)	72.46	73.98	75.30
PART	43.97	(±0.16)	43.73	43.81	43.90	0.09	(±<0.01)	0.09	0.09	0.09
RIPPER	98.72	(±0.26)	98.10	98.66	99.28	0.03	(±<0.01)	0.03	0.03	0.03
SMO	156.60	(±2.48)	147.24	148.85	171.77	0.04	(±<0.01)	0.04	0.04	0.04
MP	197.76	(±0.31)	196.67	197.20	198.54	0.27	(±<0.01)	0.27	0.27	0.28
SLR	271.65	(±0.33)	270.82	272.13	272.72	0.30	(±<0.01)	0.29	0.30	0.30
SVM*	2029.64	(±44.85)	2001.01	2021.05	2072.45	364.26	(±9.46)	354.86	365.15	375.18

Table 12.2.: Training and prediction time statistics averaged across 100 runs. The algorithms with 10 runs are denoted by *.

respectively. Moreover, SMO—which is an optimization of SVM—performs significantly faster than SVM by a factor of 13.

On the other hand, the prediction time required by the instance-based learning algorithms are very high. NNC needs seven minutes to make 68,411 predictions, while K-Star requires roughly three hours and LWL takes almost fifteen hours to predict all of them. Furthermore, SVM that requires the longest training time also needs as much time as NNC to make predictions. The prediction time of other algorithms are negligible compared to the five slowest algorithms and are almost not visible in Figure 12.3.

12.4. Discussion

This section discusses why some prediction algorithms are slow while the others are fast, why they achieve different prediction quality and which one should be chosen in specific practical applications.

12.4.1. Experimental Results

During the training process, the instance-based algorithms are very fast as they require virtually no computation and the learned instances only need to be stored in the database. However, during the prediction phase, these algorithms perform very slowly. LWL, which is the slowest algorithm during the prediction, has to build naïve Bayes models from the k-nearest neighbors of a test instance to make one prediction. This model construction dramatically slows down the prediction process. For NNC and K-Star, the distance between the test instance and all learned instances has to be computed. While Euclidean distance is used in NNC, an entropy function is used in K-Star and, as a result, requires more computation power than NNC.

ZeroR is a rule-based algorithm which performs very fast for both training and prediction phases. The reason of the fast processing is obvious as it only counts the number of instances in each class during the training and assigns the test instance to the majority class during the prediction. OneR, DT, PART, and RIPPER are other rule-based algorithms with different training and prediction speeds. These algorithms analyze the training instances and create rules according to their specific methods which causes the training time to vary. When a test instance has to be classified, it has to be checked against the rules—typically conditional statements—which is a very fast process.

MNBC, NBC, and BN are classifiers that build probabilistic models from the learned instances. MNBC creates the model by counting the occurrences of the instance features while NBC builds normal distribution models out of them. Thus, NBC is slower than MNBC as the parameters of the models have to be estimated. Besides, BN has to build both the network structure and the probabilistic models, which results in a slower training time than the other two algorithms in this category. However, for the prediction, NBC needs longer time than the other two since the class probabilities have to be computed from continuous distributions.

C4.5, REPTree, and RF are fast algorithms but still require some training time due to the tree construction phase, which searches for the best splitting nodes. Nonetheless, the prediction times of these algorithms are relatively very fast, similar to rule-based algorithms, since the splitting nodes also use conditional statements to classify instances.

SVM, which uses a hyperplane to separate the instances into classes, has the slowest training time because it requires very high computational power for quadratic programming optimization. SMO and SGD use other approaches to solve the optimization problem which significantly improve SVM and reduce both training and prediction time.

For the prediction quality, NNC is the best algorithm as we assume that when the parameters are mapped to a multi-dimension space, they do not form distinct clusters but rather spread throughout the area. During the prediction phase, a test instance is then mapped to the point where it is closest to the one with the highest similarity. NNC can thus take advantage of this similarity and correctly classify that instance. In addition, RF, C4.5, and REPTree are decision trees that achieve very high prediction quality. However, as RF contains a number of decision trees and uses voting to decide the final outcome, it tends to perform better than C4.5 and REPTree.

On the other hand, BN, MNBC, and NBC do not achieve as good prediction quality as we expected. One of our assumptions is that as the data does not form clusters, these algorithms can not create probabilistic models that clearly separate the failing and non-failing instances. This assumption also applies to SVM, SMO, and SGD which use a hyperplane to classify instances and, therefore, perform worse than our expectation.

12.4.2. Selection of Algorithms

The decision of selecting an algorithm in practice depends on the application and the constraints. Two factors that should be considered are the prediction quality and time needed for training and prediction. If the algorithm is to be trained in an offline manner and later deployed under operation, the training time can be neglected, as it can be done separately in advance. If the algorithm will be used in online learning approaches, its training time needs to be very fast to be able to process new instances and to update the prediction model at runtime. However, the prediction time of the algorithm should be considerably fast to make a prediction based on the most recent instance, before a new one arrives. When the training and prediction times are not the primary factor, the prediction quality becomes the first factor to be considered. The TPR should be taken into account when the cost of missing a failure is high. When the cost of a false alarm is high, the FPR should be considered. The overall prediction quality can be determined by F-measure value, which combines both precision and recall.

From our experiment, the algorithms which are suitable for applications that require high prediction quality without time constraint are NNC, RF, C4.5, REPTree, RIPPER, PART, and K-Star. The algorithms applicable for online learning approaches are BN and OneR since they require both short training and prediction times while maintaining relatively high prediction quality. When a low or closest-to-zero false alarm rate is desired, SMO, and SVM appear to be the best options, even though their TPRs are quite low in comparison to other algorithms.

Nonetheless, the algorithms with comparable prediction qualities may perform differently in practical applications. Even though NNC has the highest TPR in the lower range of FPR, other algorithms may outperform it when they are deployed. Therefore, the algorithms should be specifically evaluated against a certain task before being selected for real use.

12.5. Threats to Validity

One assumption we made to separate failing instances from non-failing ones is the seven-day time frame before failure. We assume that the signs of a failure are observable during this period independently from the failure type. However, this period could be shorter, or closer to the failure than seven days, and the characteristic of the captured data is actually from the non-failing drives. Consequently, the failure model could be tampered with good instances, which could cause the results to have high FPRs. Moreover, the algorithms in our experiment are set to their default configurations provided by Weka. Some algorithms that allow parameter tuning or internal modification, such as SVM with kernel trick, may perform better if their parameters are properly set to match the property of the data. Thus, our results are valid only for specific settings of the tested algorithms.

The experiment carried out in this chapter is based on a single dataset. Some characteristics embedded in the data may give advantages to some algorithms over the others. This may cause biases in the results with overly optimistic or pessimistic prediction qualities of some algorithms.

12.6. Summary

This chapter presents the evaluation of the hard drive failure prediction and answers research question RQ1.3. The results of the prediction show that different machine learning algorithms produce different prediction qualities. The best algorithms for predicting failures in hard drives based on S.M.A.R.T. data are NNC, RF, and C4.5. However, the NNC takes longer to make predictions than the other two. Thus, different parameters, e.g., available time for training and prediction phases, need to be taken into account when selecting these algorithms.

13

EVALUATION OF FAILURE
PROPAGATION PREDICTION

The previous three chapters present the evaluation results of three types of component failure prediction. This chapter presents the evaluation of the FPM which combines the time series-based failure prediction and the architectural dependency modeling.

Section 13.1 presents the research questions that will be answered in this chapter. Section 13.2 describes the experiment setup of the evaluation. Section 13.3 presents the results of the experiment. Section 13.4 provides a discussion of the results. Section 13.5 presents the threats to validity of the experiment. Section 13.6 summarizes the evaluation in this chapter.

13.1. Research Questions

This chapter focuses on evaluating the prediction quality of the Failure Propagation Model (FPM) presented in Chapter 7. Furthermore, the evaluation aims to answer the following research questions which have been previously stated in detail in Section 4.1:

- RQ2.3: Does architectural information affect the prediction quality? If yes, to which extent?

- RQ3.2: What is the prediction quality of the combined model?

- RQ3.3: What is the scalability of the combined model?

13.2. Experiment Setup

This section provides details of the system under test, the fault injection, the failure definition, and the prediction technique used in the evaluation.

13.2.1. System Under Test and Fault Injection

The evaluation of FPM is carried out based on the same dataset used to evaluate time series-based component failure prediction (Chapter 10). The dataset is collected from the RSS reader application previously described in Section 10.2.1. Fault injection includes three types of faults, namely, memory leak, system overload, and node crash.

13.2.2. Failure Definition

In Chapter 10, response time is used as a failure indicator. A request is considered a failure if the 95th percentile of the response times in a 2-minute window exceeds 1 second. This type of failure is called timing failures according to the terminology presented in Section 2.1.1. In this chapter, in addition to the timing failures, we also consider content failures. Examples of content failures are unsuccessful requests, i.e., service outage and incorrect responses. A service outage occurs when the server does not accept requests from the client. The client will wait for a reply from the server and terminate the connection after a pre-defined timeout is reached. An incorrect response occurs when the connection is accepted but the server encounters an internal problem. The problem causes the server to be unable to fulfill the request and returns an error message indicating that the request cannot be completed.

However, if the system cannot provide correct services for only one or two requests from hundreds or thousands of requests, it does not necessarily mean that the system is encountering a problem. These failures that occur infrequently may be caused by random factors, e.g., garbage collection on the server side. Thus, we use the ratio of successful requests over all requests as a measurement that represents the service status. The success ratio can be computed as

$$\text{success ratio} = \frac{\#\text{successes}}{\#\text{successes} + \#\text{failures}} \tag{13.1}$$

This ratio is computed for every 2-minute window. If this value falls below 99.99%, it is regarded that a failure has occurred in that time window.

13.2.3. Prediction Technique

As described in Chapter 7, the FPM aims to predict the propagation of the failures based on two pieces of information. The first piece of information is the dependencies between components which describes how a failure of one component can affect and propagate to other components. This information is stored in the ADM, which is extracted from the monitoring data collected from the system as described in Chapter 6.

The second piece of information is the failure probabilities of components in the system. Theses probabilities indicate the probability that a component will experience a failure in the near future. A component failure predictor is responsible for predicting this value for each individual component at runtime. The predictor used in the experiment is the time series-based component predictors described in Section 5.4. The predictor is triggered at regular interval, thus, producing a time series of failure probabilities for each component.

With these two pieces of information, the next step is to combine and use them to predict the failure propagation. The extracted ADM is first transformed to an FPM as described in Section 7.3. The FPM at this stage contains incomplete CPTs in which the component failure probabilities are missing. At runtime, the component failure probabilities obtained from the predictors in Chapter 10 are added to the CPTs. The update process is done continuously as the component failure predictors generate new component failure probabilities, as described in Section 7.4. The inference of the FPM is carried out at regular intervals in order to provide the failure probabilities of all components while keeping a low computational complexity. In this experiment, the interval is set to every two minutes according to the length of the window used to compute the failure ratio (Section 13.2.2).

13.3. Results

This section presents the result of each step of the prediction which includes the resulting ADM and FPM, and the prediction results.

13.3.1. Architectural Dependency Model

The first step in predicting failure propagation is to obtain the ADM that represents the system. To achieve this, the monitoring data in the Kieker logging format is used to create a SLAstic model of the system. The SLAstic model is then transformed into an ADM as described in Section 6.4.2. In the experiment, two instances of edges and three instances of middletiers from the RSS reader application are deployed. The size of the extracted ADM can be configured by including or excluding some components. Thus, the resulting number of components in the ADMs varies from 48 to 98. The effects of different ADM will be investigated in detail in Section 13.3.7. The complete ADMs are included in the supplementary material [Pit18].

13.3.2. Failure Propagation Model

The extracted ADM is transformed into an FPM as described in Section 7.3. An excerpt of the FPM is depicted in Figure 13.1. The FPM is composed of nodes, each of which represents one entity in the ADM. Each node has one

CPT that lists conditional probabilities for different states of the dependent components. However, the CPTs are very large and are not shown here. The complete FPMs are included in the supplementary material [Pit18].

13.3.3. Prediction Result of Memory Leak

This section presents the prediction result of the FPM in comparison with that of the time-series based predictor in Chapter 10.

The prediction results of the component failure predictors in Chapter 10 has shown that the individual predictors are able to predict the problem if that component is the root cause. In this chapter, we use FPM which takes into account the failure probabilities of other components and computes the probabilities that a failure of the memory, caused by memory leak, will cause other components to fail. Figure 13.2 depicts the prediction results of the FPM with ARIMA as component failure predictors. The figures also show the results in comparison to that of the ARIMA without FPM.

The increasing memory utilization of a business-tier instance shown in Figure 13.2a is predicted by ARIMA to reach the failure threshold at the 62th minute with a probability close to 1.0. The FPM then receives this failure probability and updates the CPT of the corresponding component. After this update, the failure probabilities of all components are recomputed by solving the FPM. The failure probability of the memory then propagates to other components that depend on it, i.e., software components deployed on that business-tier instance. There are also other instances that depend on these software components of this business-tier instance. Thus, the failure probabilities propagate to those instances as well.

The propagation of failure probabilities from the memory component to the operations of the presentation tier and the load balancer can be seen in Figures 13.2c and 13.2d. Since the memory leak is occurring in only one of the three business tier instances, the failure probability is reduced by the inference by a factor of 3. The effect of the garbage collector also causes the load average to increase, as depicted in Figure 13.2b. The failure probability from the load average further increases the failure probability of the service

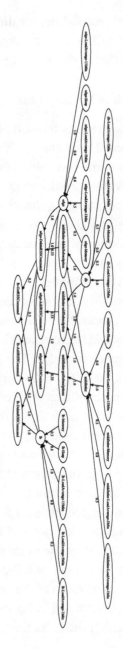

Figure 13.1.: An excerpt of the FPM of RSS reader application

at the presentation tier and the load balancer as can be seen in Figures 13.2c and 13.2d.

The results show that the memory leak causes the system to slow down which results in a sudden increase in the service response time and the service failure rate. This increase cannot be predicted by the failure predictor that considers only the response time. On the other hand, HORA considers the memory utilization of the business tier and propagates the failure probability to the service boundary. The results show that HORA can predict the service failure 10 minutes before it occurs with a failure probability of approximately 0.3. The ROC curves of HORA and the monolithic approach are depicted in Figure 13.5a.

13.3.4. Prediction Result of System Overload

Figure 13.3b depicts the increasing number of concurrent users that causes the load average of the business-tier instances to constantly increase over time. The small failure probability that is predicted by the component failure predictor of the load average is updated in the FPM and propagates to other components. Since there are three instances of the business tier and all of them get the same increasing workload, the small failure probability gets amplified and propagates to other parts. Figures 13.3c and 13.3d depict the failure probabilities of the presentation tier and the load balancer, respectively. It can be observed that the probabilities of these components are larger than that of the load average of the business tier. Furthermore, these failure probabilities are predicted in advance even before the service failures at the load balancer can be observed.

The results show that HORA can predict this type of service failure since it takes into account the dependency of the presentation tier on the business tier. On the other hand, the predictor that observes only the increase in the response time at the system boundary is not able to predict this type of service failure since the response time does not exceed the threshold. The ROC curves of both approaches are presented in Figure 13.5b.

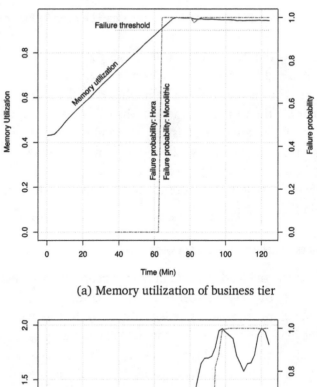

(a) Memory utilization of business tier

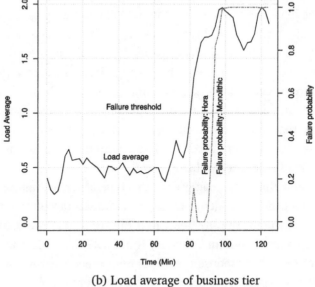

(b) Load average of business tier

Figure 13.2.: Timeline plots of selected components for memory leak scenario

13 | Evaluation of Failure Propagation Prediction

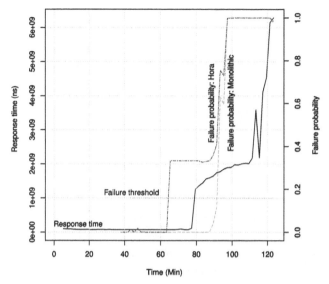

(c) Response time of presentation tier

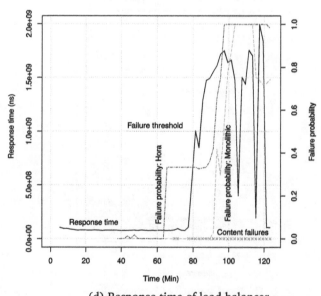

(d) Response time of load balancer

Figure 13.2.: Timeline plots of selected components for memory leak scenario (cont.)

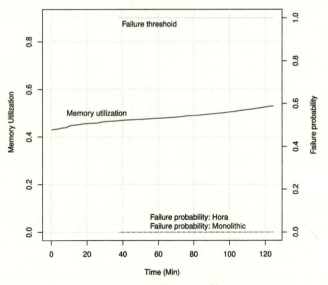

(a) Memory utilization of business tier

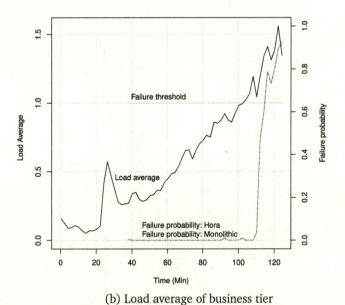

(b) Load average of business tier

Figure 13.3.: Timeline plots of selected components for system overload
scenario

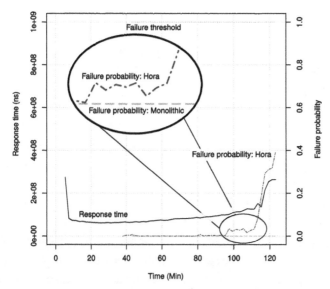

(c) Response time of presentation tier

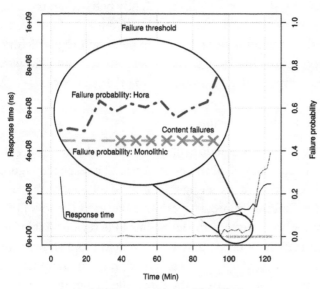

(d) Response time of load balancer

Figure 13.3.: Timeline plots of selected components for system overload
scenario (cont.)

13.3.5. Prediction Result of Node Crash

The two instances of the business tier that crash at the 90th and 95th minutes causes the remaining instance to overload and, eventually, cause the service to fail. The component failure predictor, which is ARIMA, cannot predict the first crash because it is a sudden crash and there is no preceding symptom. However, during the five-minute gap between the first and the second crash, the two remaining instance experience a higher workload and start to produce a symptom. This symptom is a noticeable increase in the load average of the remaining instances. The corresponding component failure predictors predict that there is a small probability that this can lead to a failure. This failure probability gets propagated to other dependent components by the FPM. This propagation can be seen in the failure probability of the service in Figures 13.4c and 13.4d. In contrast, the predictors that consider only the response time cannot predict the failures since they are not aware of the problem manifesting in another part of the system.

The result shows that HORA performs slightly better than the monolithic approach due to the unintended preceding symptom. However, if both instances crash at the same time, the component failure predictors would not be able to predict this failure. As a consequence, the FPM would not have any failure information to propagate to other components.

13.3.6. Overall Prediction Result

We evaluate the overall prediction quality of HORA by analyzing the combined raw prediction data of all three scenarios. The results in Figure 13.5d depicts the ROC curves of HORA against that of the monolithic approach. Although the monolithic approach performs better in the low FPR region (0–0.04), HORA outperforms it in the higher FPR region. Table 13.1 lists the prediction metrics of both approaches in detail and shows that HORA improves the overall AUC by 9.9%, compared to the monolithic approach. However, as can be observed from the table, the monolithic approach produces higher precision and accuracy that those of the HORA approach. This is

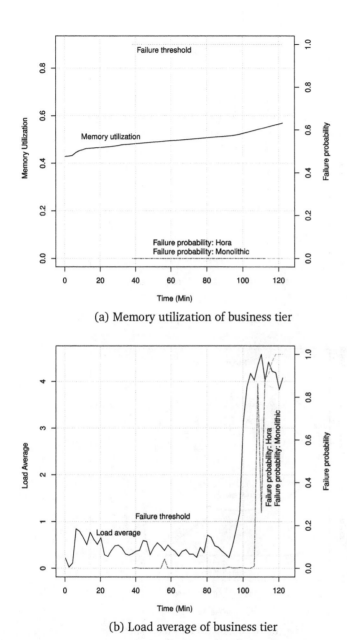

(a) Memory utilization of business tier

(b) Load average of business tier

Figure 13.4.: Timeline plots of selected components for node crash scenario

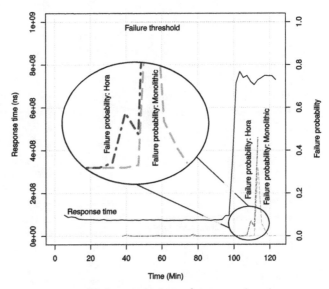

(c) Response time of presentation tier

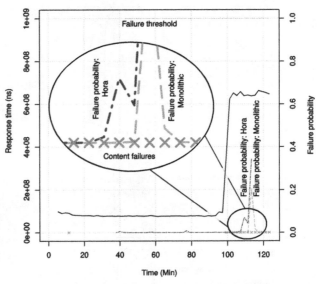

(d) Response time of load balancer

Figure 13.4.: Timeline plots of selected components for node crash scenario (cont.)

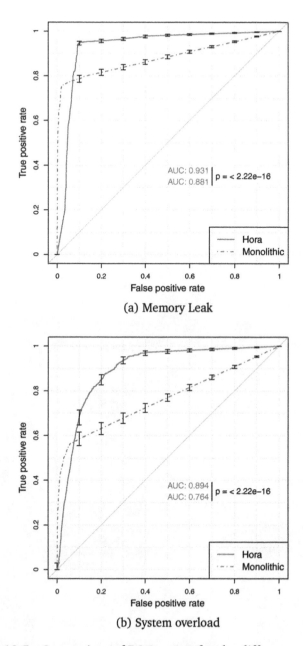

(a) Memory Leak

(b) System overload

Figure 13.5.: Comparison of ROC curves for the different types of faults

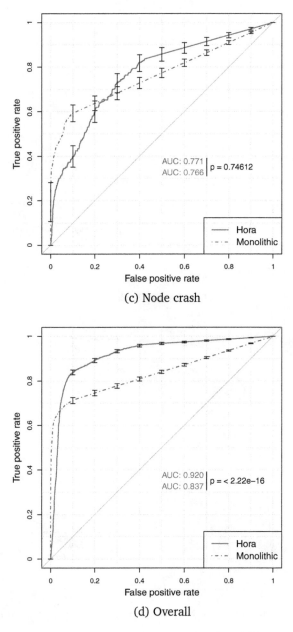

(c) Node crash

(d) Overall

Figure 13.5.: Comparison of ROC curves for the different types of faults (cont.)

Fault type	Prediction approach	Precision	Recall, TPR	FPR	Accuracy	AUC	AUC improvement	p-value
Memory leak	HORA	0.612	0.945	0.096	0.91	0.931	5.7%	$< 2.22 \times 10^{-16}$
	Monolithic	0.84	0.758	0.024	0.945	0.881		
System overload	HORA	0.181	0.876	0.216	0.789	0.894	17%	$< 2.22 \times 10^{-16}$
	Monolithic	0.352	0.564	0.059	0.92	0.764		
Node crash	HORA	0.059	0.73	0.298	0.703	0.771	$< 0.1\%$	0.746
	Monolithic	0.209	0.582	0.085	0.902	0.766		
Overall	HORA	0.419	0.833	0.091	0.903	0.92	9.9%	$< 2.22 \times 10^{-16}$
	Monolithic	0.475	0.692	0.065	0.916	0.837		

Table 13.1.: Comparison of all evaluation metrics for the different types of faults

due to the fact that HORA produces more false positives because it considers the propagation from all components in the system. A small failure probability in one of the component failure predictors can propagate through the architecture to other components. This results in a higher number of false positives. Since the calculations of precision and accuracy include false positives, these metrics of HORA are, thus, lower. Nevertheless, the number of true positives, which is used to calculate recall, of HORA is higher. This means that HORA can correctly predict more failures than the monolithic approach.

13.3.7. Architectural Dependency Model Impact

The automated extraction of the ADM allows fine-tuning of the model, e.g., adjusting the degrees of dependencies and excluding some components. This section investigates the impact of the ADM configurations on the prediction quality.

Degree of dependency—The degree of dependency between software components can be directly computed from the number of invocations described in Section 6.4.2. However, the computation of the degree of dependency from software to some hardware measures are not straightforward. For example, the load average measure contains three different values, i.e., 1-minute, 5-minute, and 15-minute averages. There are no clear guidelines what might be the effect on the operation of the physical machine if these measures exceed the threshold.

To investigate the impact of the degree of dependency, we vary the degree of dependency of the load average from 0.2 to 1.0. The results in Figure 13.6a show that the AUC, TPR, precision, and FPR remain almost constant. This is because the failure probabilities are always propagated to other parts of the system by the FPM regardless of how small they are. Those small propagated probabilities at the system boundary still provide the signs that the failure is imminent which are sufficient to trigger the warning. Therefore, we can conclude that varying the degree of dependency does not significantly affect the prediction quality.

Size of ADM— We evaluate four different ADMs which contain different numbers of architectural components:

- *Auto-Large*—The model is automatically generated and contains 98 components which include software components, as well as CPU utilization, memory utilization, swap utilization, and load average of all physical nodes.

- *Auto-Medium*—The model is automatically generated and contains 80 components which include software components, as well as memory utilization, and load average. Compared to *Auto-Large*, the CPU utilization and swap utilization are removed.

- *Auto-Small*—The model is automatically generated and contains 56 components which include only important software components, as well as memory utilization, and load average. Compared to *Auto-Medium*, the intermediate software operations are removed.

- *Manual*—The model is manually created by system experts and contains 48 components which include only the important software components, as well as memory utilization, and load average.

The complete details of these four models can be found in the supplementary material [Pit18]. The evaluation results of the models are presented in Figure 13.6b. Although all ADMs have approximately the same AUC, TPR, and FPR, the manually created ADM achieves the highest precision. This is because the automated extraction includes all components in the system whether they play a role in the failure of the whole system. Some component may not have any symptoms that contribute to the system failure. In other words, they do not help predict more failures, but rather produce more false alarms. Thus, in the manual creation of the ADM, these component can be excluded by the system expert to optimize the prediction. However, the automated extraction of the model has an advantage that it can create the ADM for a large system which is infeasible for a manual creation. Therefore, it is a trade-off between the ease in the model creation and the prediction quality.

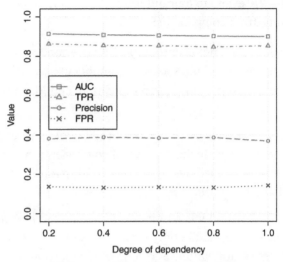

(a) Degree of dependency to load average

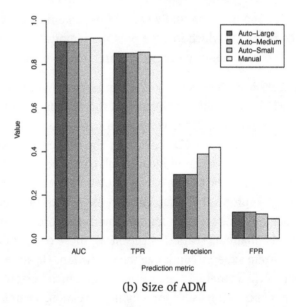

(b) Size of ADM

Figure 13.6.: Prediction quality of HORA with different ADM configurations

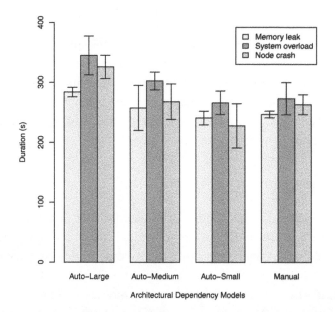

Figure 13.7.: HORA's average analysis and prediction duration (including 95% confidence interval) for 2-hour monitoring data

Nonetheless, the automatically generated model can still be fine-tuned by the system experts to produce even better prediction results.

13.3.8. Runtime Overhead

The prediction results are obtained by collecting the monitoring data from the system described in Section 10.2.1 and executing the offline analysis (Section 8.1 on a separate machine equipped with 3.10 GHz Intel Xeon E31220 running Ubuntu 12.04.5 LTS. Figure 13.7 illustrates the runtime overhead of HORA for the four different ADMs. It can be observed that the larger the model is, the more time it requires for the analysis and prediction. On average, the analysis for 2-hour monitoring data is completed in less than six minutes. This demonstrates that HORA can be deployed and make timely predictions at runtime.

It needs to be emphasized that Hora's prediction process is triggered by every new data point. For the model with 98 components, this leads to 98 predictions every 2 minutes, i.e., 5880 predictions in two hours. In this work, we focus on investigating the prediction quality of Hora rather than its prediction efficiency. Particularly, Hora has not been optimized for performance. A possible future optimization could be to configure it to make predictions at regular time intervals, e.g., every one minute.

13.4. Discussion

The FPM exploits the knowledge of the component dependencies and a set of predictors, which can predict individual component failures, to infer the failure propagation. Our results show that in the memory leak and system overload scenarios, Hora can predict the failures with high TPR. This demonstrates that the problems that develop internally can be detected early and the failure probability can be propagated to other parts of the system.

Although the results in Table 13.1 and Figure 13.5 show that Hora achieves higher TPR and higher AUC, the number of FP is also high. This results in a low precision and high FPR. In other words, the monolithic approach performs better in the low false-positive-rate range between 0 and 0.1. On the other hand, if a higher FPR is acceptable, Hora will be able to correctly predict more failures than the monolithic approach.

13.5. Threats to Validity

In the evaluation, we compare the prediction results of the Hora approach with those of the monolithic approach. Both of them employ ARIMA as component failure predictors but Hora considers the architecture of the system to propagate the failure probabilities. There are existing works of other techniques for predicting component failures. However, they are specifically applicable for different types of monitoring data or different types of components. For instance, Fronza et al. [FSS+12], Liang et al. [LZXS07b] and Salfner and Malek [SM07] employ machine learning techniques to analyze event logs and classify the system into healthy and failure states. These techniques are not directly applicable as the monitoring data obtained in our experiment is time series data. Therefore, we utilize ARIMA which is a suitable and commonly used prediction technique for this type of data.

The evaluation of the HORA approach is carried out on the RSS reader application which is based on microservice architecture. The Blue Gene/L supercompter and the computer hard drives are used to evaluate the component failure predictors (Chapters 11 and 12, respectively). However, since the data collected from Blue Gene/L supercomputer does not contain architectural information and the hard drives are individual components that do not have architectural information, they are not included in the evaluation of the HORA approach. Additionally, the prediction quality of the HORA approach is not compared to those of other prediction approaches that employ architectural information. This is because they focus on predicting other QoS attributes, e.g., performance or reliability, which makes the results not directly comparable. Furthermore, other online failure prediction approaches either focus on predicting the failures of one specific system, e.g., event log-based failure prediction, and cannot be applied to other systems, or they do not consider the architecture of the system in the prediction.

13.6. Summary

This chapter presents the evaluation of the Failure Propagation Model (FPM) and answers research questions RQ2.3, RQ3.2, and RQ3.3. The evaluation results show that the FPM, which is the model that combines component failure prediction and architectural knowledge, outperforms monolithic failure prediction and can improve the overall AUC by 9.9%. Different configurations of the ADM, namely the degree of dependency and the size, are investigated and the results show that they have minimal impacts on the prediction quality. Lastly, the evaluation of runtime overhead shows that the HORA approach can make predictions in a timely manner and can be applied to predict failures at runtime.

Part IV.

Conclusions and Future Work

14

CONCLUSIONS

Failures in software systems usually develop inside the system and propagate to the boundary. Existing online failure prediction approaches do not explicitly consider the software system architecture and failure propagation paths. They see the system as a monolith and make predictions based only on the available measurements, such as response time or memory utilization.

This thesis presents HORA, an architecture-aware approach for online failure prediction in software systems, which combines the traditional failure prediction with architectural knowledge to provide architecture-aware failure predictions. The approach is divided into three parts, which are component failure prediction, architectural dependency modeling, and failure propagation modeling.

Component Failure Prediction In contrast to predicting the failure of the whole system, the HORA approach focuses on predicting the failure of each individual component in the system based on the monitoring data. However, since a system is composed of different types of hardware and software components, different types of data that reflects component status can be obtained at runtime. Therefore, different prediction techniques can be selected and applied to each type of data independently from the others. This allows the predictors to be reusable and optimized for the best prediction quality. In this thesis, three different types of monitoring data are considered. The first type of data is time series which is collected from resource utilization and software method response time. The second type is event logs collected from a supercomputer. The third type is hard drive S.M.A.R.T. data. The results show that different prediction techniques can be applied to different types of data and can predict component failures with high prediction quality.

Architectural Dependency Modeling   The Architectural Dependency Model (ADM) introduced in this thesis stores information regarding the dependencies between components and how much they depend on each other. This information represents how, and to which extent, a failure of one component can propagate to the others. The ADM can be created manually by system experts that have detailed knowledge about the system structure and behavior. It can also be created automatically by analyzing the monitoring data that is collected from APM tools, such as Kieker. In this thesis, the ADM is obtained by an automated transformation from the SLAstic model which contains the structural and behavioral information of the system. The SLAstic is, in turn, automatically extracted from Kieker monitoring logs obtained from the system at runtime. Moreover, the extraction of an ADM from Kieker monitoring data is also presented. Thus, the resulting ADM can represent the component dependencies based on the structure and behavior of the actual system at runtime.

Failure Propagation Modeling   The FPM is the model that combines the results of component failure predictors and the ADM to infer the failure probabilities of the components and the whole system based on the architectural knowledge. The ADM presented in the previous step is transformed into an FPM, which employs Bayesian network theory to model the failure propagation. The prediction results from component failure predictors in the first step are incorporated into the model and updated periodically so that the model represents the actual status of the system. In the last step, the model is solved at regular intervals to obtain the failure probability of each component, as well as the whole system and the provided service. This approach allows a higher degree of modularity as different failure prediction techniques can be applied and reused among similar types of components. The evaluation shows that HORA can improve online failure prediction for software systems by explicitly considering architectural knowledge. The results show that HORA provides a significantly higher prediction quality than the monolithic approach and can improve the overall AUC by 9.9%.

15

FUTURE WORK

This chapter discusses the future work of the HORA approach introduced in this thesis.

Component Failure Prediction   The types of data considered in component failure prediction are time series, event logs, and S.M.A.R.T. data. These types of data are collected from CPU, software components, logs files of supercomputer, and hard drives. There are other components that provide the same types of data, e.g., network utilization, disk utilization, application-level logs. These sources of information can provide more information that may help predicting the failures. However, further investigation is required to discover the relationship between these components and the failure of the system. Moreover, suitable prediction techniques for these components need to be investigated and optimized to produce high prediction quality.

Architectural Dependency Modeling   The ADM in this thesis is automatically transformed from a SLAstic model which is extracted from the Kieker monitoring data. The extraction can be extended to support other types of architectural models, such as PCM or Descartes.

The extraction of the ADM can also be extended to support architectural changes at runtime. The possibility of an automatic architectural change detection, which triggers the extraction of a new ADM, may be investigated. This will allow the ADM to be kept synchronized with the actual architecture of the system.

Failure Propagation Modeling   The FPM in this thesis employs Bayesian network theory to represent the propagation of the failures. The Bayesian network is chosen because it can model the relationships between components using its CPTs. However, there might be other types of models that are also suitable for this purpose. Further investigation is needed to evaluate their suitability and the prediction quality.

The current limitation of the FPM is that the lead time of all component failure predictors need to have the same value. In our evaluation, this value is set to ten minutes. In the future work, an extension of the Bayesian network can be investigated so that different lead times for different components can be employed. This will allow more flexibility when selecting and optimizing component failure predictors as different techniques and different types of components may produce different prediction qualities with different lead times. However, this means that the final result of failure prediction will no longer be a probability and the expected time of occurrence. The result would become a failure probability distribution over time. The existing evaluation method will no longer suffice since it only considers one value of failure probability. A new way of evaluating the prediction quality also needs to be investigated to handle probability distributions as prediction results.

Furthermore, the architectural patterns that aim to improve system reliability can also be integrated into the FPM. For example, a circuit breaker is a pattern that aims to prevent a failure of one component from propagating to the next component [Nyg18]. More research is required to investigate the effects of such patterns on the failure propagation and how these patterns can be modeled in the FPM.

Failure Diagnosis   At runtime, when a failure is predicted, the next step in proactive fault management is to diagnose the problem. The diagnosis is carried out to gather more information so that the countermeasures can be planned and applied effectively. One example of failure diagnosis is fault localization. A fault that causes a failure that propagates to the system boundary will usually cause other components along the propagation path to fail. The fault localization needs to consider the architecture of the system and trace it back from the system boundary to the origin of the fault. In the HORA approach, this information is already available in the ADM. The results of the component failure predictors can be linked with the ADM to provide a failure propagation diagram. The diagram can assist the developers or operators to better visualize and understand the root cause and the propagation of the failures.

Automatic Failure Avoidance   After a failure has been predicted and the location of the fault has been identified, countermeasures can be applied to prevent the failure from occurring. The information which is available from the diagnosis step can help in the planning and execution of the preventive maintenance. For example, if one instance of a microservice is predicted to fail in the near future, a new instance can be spawned and the problematic instance can be terminated before it causes a failure. Another example is when a new version of a microservice, which contains a software bug, has been deployed to a production environment. If online failure prediction can predict that all instances of the new version are going to cause a failure, a countermeasure can trigger a rollback mechanism that reverts all instances back to an older version. In addition to the execution of a countermeasure, if the lead time of the failure prediction is sufficiently long, different countermeasures can be investigated and simulated. This will allow the best countermeasure to be chosen and applied to produce the best result.

Bibliography

[AAA+02] N.R. Adiga, G. Almási, G.S. Almasi, Y. Aridor, R. Barik, D. Beece, R. Bellofatto, G. Bhanot, R. Bickford, M. Blumrich, et al. "An overview of the BlueGene/L supercomputer." In: *Proceedings of ACM/IEEE Conference on Supercomputing (ICS)*. IEEE. 2002, pp. 60–60 (cit. on p. 180).

[AAKR13] H.J. Abed, A. Al-Fuqaha, B. Khan, A. Rayes. "Efficient failure prediction in autonomic networks based on trend and frequency analysis of anomalous patterns." In: *International Journal of Network Management*. Vol. 23. 3. May 2013, pp. 186–213 (cit. on p. 52).

[ACC+14] D. Ardagna, G. Casale, M. Ciavotta, J.F. Pérez, W. Wang. "Quality-of-service in cloud computing: modeling techniques and their applications." In: *Journal of Internet Services and Applications* 5.1 (Sept. 2014), p. 11 (cit. on p. 39).

[ACG11] A. Amin, A. Colman, L. Grunske. "Using automated control charts for the runtime evaluation of qos attributes." In: *Proceedings of the 13th International Symposium on High-Assurance Systems Engineering (HASE)*. 2011, pp. 299–306 (cit. on p. 52).

[ACG12] A. Amin, A. Colman, L. Grunske. "An approach to forecasting QoS attributes of web services based on ARIMA and GARCH models." In: *Proceedings of the 19th IEEE International Conference on Web Services (ICWS)*. 2012, pp. 74–81 (cit. on pp. 2, 52, 53).

[AGK+02] L. Abeni, A. Goel, C. Krasic, J. Snow, J. Walpole. "A measurement-based analysis of the real-time performance of linux." In: *Proceedings of the 8th IEEE Real-Time and Embedded Technology and Applications Symposium (RTAS)*. 2002, pp. 133–142 (cit. on p. 38).

[AKA91]   D. W. Aha, D. Kibler, M. K. Albert. "Instance-based learning algorithms."
            In: *Machine Learning* 6 (1 1991), pp. 37–66 (cit. on p. 27).

[ALRL04]   A. Avizienis, J.-C. Laprie, B. Randell, C. Landwehr. "Basic concepts and
            taxonomy of dependable and secure computing." In: *IEEE Transactions
            on Dependable and Secure Computing.* Vol. 1. 1. Jan. 2004, pp. 11–33
            (cit. on pp. 1, 2, 12–15, 57, 162).

[AMS97]   C. G. Atkeson, A. W. Moore, S. Schaal. "Locally Weighted Learning." In:
            Artificial Intelligence Review 11 (1-5 1997), pp. 11–73 (cit. on p. 28).

[ANS+04]   W. Abdelmoez, D. M. Nassar, M. Shereshevsky, N. Gradetsky, R. Gun-
            nalan, H. H. Ammar, B. Yu, A. Mili. "Error propagation in software
            architectures." In: *Proceedings of the 10th International Symposium on
            Software Metrics.* Sept. 2004, pp. 384–393 (cit. on p. 5).

[ARK+10]   A. Al-Fuqaha, A. Rayes, D. Kountanis, H. Abed, A. Kamel, R. Salih. "Pre-
            diction of performance degradation in telecommunication networks
            using joint clustering and association analysis techniques." In: *GLOBE-
            COM Workshops (GC Wkshps).* 2010, pp. 534–538 (cit. on p. 50).

[ATBG10]   J. Alonso, J. Torres, J. L. Berral, R. Gavalda. "Adaptive on-line soft-
            ware aging prediction based on machine learning." In: *Proceedings of
            IEEE/IFIP International Conference on Dependable Systems and Networks
            (DSN).* 2010, pp. 507–516 (cit. on p. 49).

[ATG09]   J. Alonso, J. Torres, R. Gavalda. "Predicting web server crashes: A case
            study in comparing prediction algorithms." In: *Proceedings of the 5th
            International Conference on Autonomic and Autonomous Systems (ICAS).*
            IEEE. 2009, pp. 264–269 (cit. on p. 49).

[BBEM15]   Y. Brun, J. young Bang, G. Edwards, N. Medvidovic. "Self-adapting
            reliability in distributed software systems." In: *IEEE Transactions on
            Software Engineering* 41.8 (2015), pp. 764–780 (cit. on p. 2).

[BCK12]   L. Bass, P. Clements, R. Kazman. *Software Architecture in Practice.* 3rd.
            Addison-Wesley Professional, 2012 (cit. on p. 5).

[BDIS04]   S. Balsamo, A. Di Marco, P. Inverardi, M. Simeoni. "Model-Based
            Performance Prediction in Software Development: A Survey." In: *IEEE
            Transaction on Software Engineering* 30.5 (May 2004), pp. 295–310
            (cit. on p. 56).

[BG04]   M. A. Babar, I. Gorton. "Comparison of scenario-based software architecture evaluation methods." In: *Proceedings of the 11th Asia-Pacific Software Engineering Conference (APSEC)*. IEEE. 2004, pp. 600–607 (cit. on p. 56).

[BHK14]   F. Brosig, N. Huber, S. Kounev. "Architecture-level software performance abstractions for online performance prediction." In: *Science of Computer Programming* 90 (2014), pp. 71–92 (cit. on p. 101).

[BHW+15]   A. Brunnert, A. van Hoorn, F. Willnecker, A. Danciu, W. Hasselbring, C. Heger, N. Herbst, P. Jamshidi, R. Jung, J. von Kistowski, A. Koziolek, J. Kroß, S. Spinner, C. Vögele, J. Walter, A. Wert. *Performance-oriented DevOps: A Research Agenda*. Tech. rep. SPEC-RG-2015-01. SPEC Research Group — DevOps Performance Working Group, Standard Performance Evaluation Corporation (SPEC), Aug. 2015 (cit. on p. 39).

[Bie12]   T. C. Bielefeld. "Online performance anomaly detection for large-scale software systems." MA thesis. Kiel University, 2012 (cit. on p. 139).

[Bis06]   C. M. Bishop. *Pattern Recognition and Machine Learning*. Springer, 2006 (cit. on pp. 22, 28, 124, 132).

[BJM+05]   O. Babaoglu, M. Jelasity, A. Montresor, C. Fetzer, S. Leonardi, A. v. Moorsel, M. v. Steen. *Self-star Properties in Complex Information Systems: Conceptual and Practical Foundations*. Springer, 2005 (cit. on p. 14).

[BKR09]   S. Becker, H. Koziolek, R. Reussner. "The Palladio Component Model for Model-driven Performance Prediction." In: *Journal of Systems and Software* 82.1 (Jan. 2009), pp. 3–22 (cit. on pp. 39, 57, 101).

[BLM+12]   R. Baldoni, G. Lodi, L. Montanari, G. Mariotta, M. Rizzuto. "Online black-box failure prediction for mission critical distributed systems." In: *Computer Safety, Reliability, and Security*. Springer, 2012, pp. 185–197 (cit. on pp. 2, 50).

[BMR15]   R. Baldoni, L. Montanari, M. Rizzuto. "On-line failure prediction in safety-critical systems." In: *Future Generation Computer Systems* 45 (2015), pp. 123–132 (cit. on p. 50).

[Bot10]   L. Bottou. "Large-Scale Machine Learning with Stochastic Gradient Descent." In: *Proceedings of the 19th International Conference on Computational Statistics (COMPSTAT)*. Springer, Aug. 2010, pp. 177–187 (cit. on p. 27).

[Bra97]   A. P. Bradley. "The use of the area under the ROC curve in the evaluation of machine learning algorithms." In: *Pattern Recognition* 30.7 (1997), pp. 1145–1159 (cit. on p. 152).

[Bre01]   L. Breiman. "Random Forests." In: *Machine Learning* 45 (1 2001), pp. 5–32 (cit. on p. 25).

[Bro12]   F. Brosch. *Integrated software architecture-based reliability prediction for IT systems*. Vol. 9. KIT Scientific Publishing, 2012 (cit. on p. 57).

[BZJ04]   M. A. Babar, L. Zhu, R. Jeffery. "A framework for classifying and comparing software architecture evaluation methods." In: *Proceedings of 2004 Australian Software Engineering Conference (ASWEC)*. 2004, pp. 309–318 (cit. on p. 56).

[CAS12]   T. Chalermarrewong, T. Achalakul, S. C. W. See. "Failure Prediction of Data Centers Using Time Series and Fault Tree Analysis." In: *Proceedings of the IEEE 18th International Conference on Parallel and Distributed Systems (ICPADS)*. 2012, pp. 794–799 (cit. on p. 57).

[CDC10]   B. Cavallo, M. Di Penta, G. Canfora. "An empirical comparison of methods to support QoS-aware service selection." In: *Proceedings of the 2nd International Workshop on Principles of Engineering Service-Oriented Systems (PESOS)*. ACM. 2010, pp. 64–70 (cit. on pp. 2, 52).

[CDI11]   V. Cortellessa, A. Di Marco, P. Inverardi. *Model-based software performance analysis*. Springer Science & Business Media, 2011 (cit. on p. 47).

[CE09]   B. Chelf, C. Ebert. "Ensuring the Integrity of Embedded Software with Static Code Analysis." In: *IEEE Software* 26.3 (May 2009), pp. 96–99 (cit. on p. 106).

[CG07]   V. Cortellessa, V. Grassi. "A modeling approach to analyze the impact of error propagation on reliability of component-based systems." In: *Proceedings of International Symposium on Component-Based Software Engineering (CBSE)*. Springer. 2007, pp. 140–156 (cit. on pp. 2, 5, 57).

[CGK+11]   R. Calinescu, L. Grunske, M. Z. Kwiatkowska, R. Mirandola, G. Tamburrelli. "Dynamic QoS Management and Optimization in Service-Based Systems." In: *IEEE Transaction on Software Engineering* 37.3 (2011), pp. 387–409 (cit. on p. 2).

[CH10]   A. Clemm, M. Hartwig. "NETradamus: A forecasting system for system event messages." In: *Proceedings of Network Operations and Management Symposium (NOMS)*. IEEE. 2010, pp. 623–630 (cit. on p. 53).

[CH92]   S. le Cessie, J. van Houwelingen. "Ridge Estimators in Logistic Regression." In: *Applied Statistics* 41.1 (1992), pp. 191–201 (cit. on p. 27).

[Che80]   R. C. Cheung. "A User-Oriented Software Reliability Model." In: *IEEE Transaction on Software Engineering* 6.2 (Mar. 1980), pp. 118–125 (cit. on p. 57).

[CKF+04]   G. Candea, S. Kawamoto, Y. Fujiki, G. Friedman, A. Fox. "Microreboot— A technique for cheap recovery." In: *Proceedings of Symposium on Operating Systems Design & Implementation (OSDI)*. 2004, pp. 31–44 (cit. on p. 2).

[CLL+12]   L. Cui, B. Li, J. Li, J. Hardy, L. Liu. "Software aging in virtualized environments: detection and prediction." In: *Proceedings of the 18th International Conference on Parallel and Distributed Systems (ICPADS)*. IEEE. 2012, pp. 718–719 (cit. on p. 52).

[CNH+13]   P. Capelastegui, A. Navas, F. Huertas, R. Garcia-Carmona, J. C. Dueñas. "An online failure prediction system for private IaaS platforms." In: *Proceedings of the 2nd International Workshop on Dependability Issues in Cloud Computing (DISCCO)*. ACM. 2013, p. 4 (cit. on p. 58).

[Coh95]   W. W. Cohen. "Fast Effective Rule Induction." In: *Proceedings of the 12th International Conference on Machine Learning (ICML)*. Morgan Kaufmann, 1995, pp. 115–123 (cit. on p. 26).

[CT95]   J. G. Cleary, L. E. Trigg. "K*: An Instance-based Learner Using an Entropic Distance Measure." In: *Proceedings of the 12th International Conference on Machine Learning (ICML)*. Morgan Kaufmann, 1995, pp. 108–114 (cit. on p. 28).

[CV95]   C. Cortes, V. Vapnik. "Support-vector networks." In: *Machine Learning* 20 (3 1995), pp. 273–297 (cit. on p. 26).

[DDC88]   E. R. DeLong, D. M. DeLong, D. L. Clarke-Pearson. "Comparing the Areas under Two or More Correlated Receiver Operating Characteristic Curves: A Nonparametric Approach." In: *Biometrics* 44.3 (1988), pp. 837–845 (cit. on p. 154).

[DHH+17]   T. F. Düllmann, R. Heinrich, A. v. Hoorn, T. Pitakrat, J. Walter, F. Willnecker. "CASPA: A platform for comparability of architecture-based software performance engineering approaches." In: *International Conference on Software Architecture Workshops (ICSAW)*. 2017, pp. 294–297 (cit. on pp. IX, 141).

[ECHS08]   B. Eckart, X. Chen, X. He, S. L. Scott. "Failure prediction models for proactive fault tolerance within storage systems." In: *Proceedings of IEEE International Symposium on Modeling, Analysis and Simulation of Computers and Telecommunication Systems (MASCOTS)*. IEEE. 2008, pp. 1–8 (cit. on p. 50).

[EDB08a]   H. El-Shishiny, S. S. Deraz, O. B. Badreddin. "Mining software aging: A neural network approach." In: *Proceedings of IEEE Symposium on Computers and Communications (ISCC)*. IEEE. 2008, pp. 182–187 (cit. on p. 49).

[EDB08b]   H. El-Shishiny, S. Deraz, O. Bahy. "Mining software aging patterns by artificial neural networks." In: *Artificial Neural Networks in Pattern Recognition*. Springer, 2008, pp. 252–262 (cit. on p. 49).

[Faw06]   T. Fawcett. "An introduction to ROC analysis." In: *Pattern Recognition Letters* 27.8 (2006), pp. 861–874 (cit. on p. 152).

[FFH08]   E. W. Fulp, G. A. Fink, J. N. Haack. "Predicting Computer System Failures Using Support Vector Machines." In: *Proceedings of the First USENIX Conference on Analysis of System Logs*. Vol. 8. 2008, pp. 5–5 (cit. on p. 54).

[FGG97]   N. Friedman, D. Geiger, M. Goldszmidt. "Bayesian Network Classifiers." In: *Machine Learning* 29 (2-3 1997), pp. 131–163 (cit. on p. 24).

[FGH06]   P. H. Feiler, D. P. Gluch, J. J. Hudak. *The architecture analysis & design language (AADL): An introduction*. Tech. rep. Carnegie-Mellon Univ Pittsburgh PA Software Engineering Inst, 2006 (cit. on p. 38).

[FGP12]   J. Fullop, A. Gainaru, J. Plutchak. "Real time analysis and event prediction engine." In: *Proceedings of the Cray User Group meeting.* 2012 (cit. on p. 55).

[FHP03]   E. Frank, M. Hall, B. Pfahringer. "Locally weighted naive Bayes." In: *Proceedings of the 19th Conference on Uncertainty in Artificial Intelligence (UAI).* San Francisco, CA, USA: Morgan Kaufmann, 2003, pp. 249–256 (cit. on p. 28).

[FHT00]   J. Friedman, T. Hastie, R. Tibshirani. "Additive logistic regression: a statistical view of boosting." In: *The annals of statistics* 28.2 (2000), pp. 337–407 (cit. on p. 27).

[Fow02]   M. Fowler. *Patterns of Enterprise Application Architecture.* Addison Wesley, 2002 (cit. on p. 3).

[FRZ+12]   X. Fu, R. Ren, J. Zhan, W. Zhou, Z. Jia, G. Lu. "LogMaster: mining event correlations in logs of large-scale cluster systems." In: *Proceedings of the 31st Symposium on Reliable Distributed Systems (SRDS).* IEEE. 2012, pp. 71–80 (cit. on p. 54).

[FS98]   Y. Freund, R. E. Schapire. "Large margin classification using the perceptron algorithm." In: *Proceedings of the 11th Annual Conference on Computational Learning Theory (COLT).* ACM, 1998, pp. 209–217 (cit. on p. 27).

[FSS+12]   I. Fronza, A. Sillitti, G. Succi, M. Terho, J. Vlasenko. "Failure prediction based on log files using Random Indexing and Support Vector Machines." In: *Journal of Systems and Software* (2012), pp. 1–10 (cit. on pp. 55, 226).

[FW98]   E. Frank, I. H. Witten. "Generating Accurate Rule Sets Without Global Optimization." In: *Proceedings of the 15th International Conference on Machine Learning (ICML).* Morgan Kaufmann, 1998, pp. 144–151 (cit. on p. 26).

[GCF+11]   A. Gainaru, F. Cappello, J. Fullop, S. Trausan-Matu, W. Kramer. "Adaptive event prediction strategy with dynamic time window for large-scale HPC systems." In: *Managing Large-scale Systems via the Analysis of System Logs and the Application of Machine Learning Techniques.* ACM. 2011, p. 4 (cit. on p. 55).

[GCK+16]   S. Ganguly, A. Consul, A. Khan, B. Bussone, J. Richards, A. Miguel. "A Practical Approach to Hard Disk Failure Prediction in Cloud Platforms: Big Data Model for Failure Management in Datacenters." In: *Proceedings of the 2nd International Conference on Big Data Computing Service and Applications (BigDataService)*. IEEE. 2016, pp. 105–116 (cit. on p. 51).

[Ge11]   W. Ge. "Prediction-based failure management for supercomputers." PhD thesis. University of Manchester, 2011 (cit. on p. 55).

[GH08]   L. Grunske, J. Han. "A comparative study into architecture-based safety evaluation methodologies using AADL's error annex and failure propagation models." In: *Proceedings of the 11th High Assurance Systems Engineering Symposium (HASE)*. 2008, pp. 283–292 (cit. on p. 56).

[GJW+10]   J. Guo, Y. Ju, Y. Wang, X. Li, B. Zhang. "The prediction of software aging trend based on user intention." In: *Proceedings of Youth Conference on Information Computing and Telecommunications (YC-ICT)*. 2010, pp. 206–209 (cit. on p. 49).

[GMW10]   D. Garlan, R. Monroe, D. Wile. "Acme: An Architecture Description Interchange Language." In: *CASCON First Decade High Impact Papers*. Riverton, NJ, USA: IBM Corp., 2010, pp. 159–173 (cit. on p. 38).

[GPYC08]   X. Gu, S. Papadimitriou, P. S. Yu, S.-P. Chang. "Online failure forecast for fault-tolerant data stream processing." In: *Proceedings of the 24th International Conference on Data Engineering (ICDE)*. IEEE. 2008, pp. 1388–1390 (cit. on p. 51).

[Gru07]   L. Grunske. "Early quality prediction of component-based systems - A generic framework." In: *Journal of Systems and Software* 80.5 (2007), pp. 678–686 (cit. on p. 56).

[GS14]   A. Gosain, G. Sharma. "A Survey of Dynamic Program Analysis Techniques and Tools." In: *Proceedings of the 3rd International Conference on Frontiers of Intelligent Computing: Theory and Applications (FICTA)*. Vol. 1. 2014, pp. 113–122 (cit. on p. 107).

[GT01]   K. Goševa-Popstojanova, K. S. Trivedi. "Architecture-based approach to reliability assessment of software systems." In: *Performance Evaluation* 45.2–3 (2001). Performance Validation of Software Systems, pp. 179–204 (cit. on p. 56).

[GVVT98]   S. Garg, A. Van Moorsel, K. Vaidyanathan, K. S. Trivedi. "A methodology for detection and estimation of software aging." In: *Proceedings of the 9th International Symposium on Software Reliability Engineering (ISSRE)*. IEEE. 1998, pp. 283–292 (cit. on p. 49).

[GW09]   X. Gu, H. Wang. "Online anomaly prediction for robust cluster systems." In: *Proceedings of the 25th International Conference on Data Engineering (ICDE)*. IEEE. 2009, pp. 1000–1011 (cit. on p. 51).

[GZF11a]   Q. Guan, Z. Zhang, S. Fu. "Ensemble of bayesian predictors for autonomic failure management in cloud computing." In: *Proceedings of the 20th International Conference on Computer Communications and Networks (ICCCN)*. IEEE. 2011, pp. 1–6 (cit. on p. 52).

[GZF11b]   Q. Guan, Z. Zhang, S. Fu. "Proactive failure management by integrated unsupervised and semi-supervised learning for dependable cloud systems." In: *Proceedings of the 6th International Conference on Availability, Reliability and Security (ARES)*. IEEE. 2011, pp. 83–90 (cit. on p. 52).

[GZF12]   Q. Guan, Z. Zhang, S. Fu. "Ensemble of bayesian predictors and decision trees for proactive failure management in cloud computing systems." In: *Journal of Communications* 7.1 (2012), pp. 52–61 (cit. on pp. 51, 52).

[GZL+08]   J. Gu, Z. Zheng, Z. Lan, J. White, E. Hocks, B.-H. Park. "Dynamic meta-learning for failure prediction in large-scale systems: A case study." In: *Proceedings of the 37th International Conference on Parallel Processing (ICPP)*. IEEE. 2008, pp. 157–164 (cit. on p. 53).

[Hal08]   E. Halili. *Apache JMeter*. Packt Publishing, 2008 (cit. on p. 160).

[Hay99]   S. S. Haykin. *Neural Networks: A Comprehensive Foundation*. Prentice Hall, 1999 (cit. on p. 27).

[HBS+17]   N. Huber, F. Brosig, S. Spinner, S. Kounev, M. Bähr. "Model-Based Self-Aware Performance and Resource Management Using the Descartes Modeling Language." In: *IEEE Transactions on Software Engineering* 43.5 (May 2017), pp. 432–452 (cit. on p. 57).

[HHMO17]   C. Heger, A. van Hoorn, M. Mann, D. Okanović. "Application Performance Management: State of the Art and Challenges for the Future." In: *Proceedings of the 8th ACM/SPEC on International Conference on Performance Engineering (ICPE)*. ACM, 2017, pp. 429–432 (cit. on pp. 40, 41).

[HJS01]   M. Hiller, A. Jhumka, N. Suri. "An approach for analysing the propagation of data errors in software." In: *Proceedings of International Conference on Dependable Systems and Networks (DSN)*. IEEE. 2001, pp. 161–170 (cit. on pp. 2, 5).

[HL05]   J. Huang, C. X. Ling. "Using AUC and accuracy in evaluating learning algorithms." In: *IEEE Transactions on Knowledge and Data Engineering* 17.3 (Mar. 2005), pp. 299–310 (cit. on p. 152).

[Hol93]   R. C. Holte. "Very Simple Classification Rules Perform Well on Most Commonly Used Datasets." In: *Machine Learning* 11 (1 1993), pp. 63–90 (cit. on p. 25).

[Hoo14]   A. van Hoorn. "Model-driven online capacity management for componet based software systems." PhD thesis. 2014 (cit. on pp. 7, 41, 42, 44, 46, 101, 107, 115, 116, 118, 120).

[HRS+08]   M. Hibler, R. Ricci, L. Stoller, J. Duerig, S. Guruprasad, T. Stack, K. Webb, J. Lepreau. "Large-scale Virtualization in the Emulab Network Testbed." In: *USENIX Annual Technical Conference*. 2008, pp. 113–128 (cit. on p. 161).

[HSM01]   D. J. Hand, P. Smyth, H. Mannila. *Principles of Data Mining*. MIT Press, 2001 (cit. on p. 181).

[HTF01]   T. Hastie, R. Tibshirani, J. Friedman. *The Elements of Statistical Learning*. Springer, 2001 (cit. on p. 23).

[HWH12]   A. van Hoorn, J. Waller, W. Hasselbring. "Kieker: A framework for application performance monitoring and dynamic software analysis." In: *Proceedings of the 3rd ACM/SPEC International Conference on Performance Engineering (ICPE)*. ACM. 2012, pp. 247–248 (cit. on pp. 7, 44, 107, 136, 139, 140, 161).

[IEE95]   IEEE 610.10-1994. "IEEE Standard Glossary of Computer Hardware Terminology." In: *IEEE Std 610.10-1994* (1995), pp. i– (cit. on p. 35).

[ISO11]   ISO/IEC/IEEE 42010:2011(E). "ISO/IEC/IEEE Systems and software engineering – Architecture description." In: *ISO/IEC/IEEE 42010:2011 (E) (Revision of ISO/IEC 42010:2007 and IEEE Std 1471-2000)* (Dec. 2011), pp. 1–46 (cit. on pp. 33, 37).

[IV14]   I. Irrera, M. Vieira. "A practical approach for generating failure data for assessing and comparing failure prediction algorithms." In: *Proceedings of the 20th Pacific Rim International Symposium on Dependable Computing (PRDC)*. IEEE. 2014, pp. 86–95 (cit. on p. 177).

[JS05]   A. Johansson, N. Suri. "Error propagation profiling of operating systems." In: *Proceedings of International Conference on Dependable Systems and Networks (DSN)*. IEEE. 2005, pp. 86–95 (cit. on p. 2).

[KBH14]   S. Kounev, F. Brosig, N. Huber. *The Descartes Modeling Language*. Tech. rep. Department of Computer Science, University of Wuerzburg, Oct. 2014, p. 91 (cit. on p. 39).

[KFPH05]   A. M. Kibriya, E. Frank, B. Pfahringer, G. Holmes. "Multinomial Naive Bayes for Text Categorization Revisited." In: *AI 2004: Advances in Artificial Intelligence*. Vol. 3339. LNCS. Springer, 2005, pp. 488–499 (cit. on p. 24).

[KHH+01]   G. Kiczales, E. Hilsdale, J. Hugunin, M. Kersten, J. Palm, W. G. Griswold. "An overview of AspectJ." In: *European Conference on Object-Oriented Programming*. Springer. 2001, pp. 327–354 (cit. on p. 138).

[Koh95]   R. Kohavi. "The power of decision tables." In: *Proceedings of the 8th European Conference on Machine Learning (ECML)*. Vol. 912. LNCS. Springer, 1995, pp. 174–189 (cit. on p. 26).

[Koz10]   H. Koziolek. "Performance evaluation of component-based software systems: A survey." In: *Performance Evaluation* 67.8 (2010). Special Issue on Software and Performance, pp. 634–658 (cit. on p. 56).

[KWTI15]   T. Kimura, A. Watanabe, T. Toyono, K. Ishibashi. "Proactive failure detection learning generation patterns of large-scale network logs." In: *Proceedings of the 11th International Conference on Network and Service Management (CNSM)*. IEEE. 2015, pp. 8–14 (cit. on p. 56).

[LD05]   D. Lowd, P. Domingos. "Naive Bayes models for probability estimation." In: *Proceedings of the 22nd International Conference on Machine Learning (ICML)*. ACM, 2005, pp. 529–536 (cit. on p. 24).

[LHF05]   N. Landwehr, M. Hall, E. Frank. "Logistic Model Trees." In: 95.1-2 (2005), pp. 161–205 (cit. on p. 27).

[LL06]   Y. Li, Z. Lan. "Exploit failure prediction for adaptive fault-tolerance in cluster computing." In: *Proceedings of the 6th IEEE International Symposium on Cluster Computing and the Grid (CCGRID)*. Vol. 1. IEEE. 2006, 8–pp (cit. on p. 2).

[LMP08]   D. Lorenzoli, L. Mariani, M. Pezzè. "Automatic generation of software behavioral models." In: *Proceedings of the 30th International Conference on Software engineering (ICSE)*. ACM. 2008, pp. 501–510 (cit. on pp. 101, 107).

[LMRD10] P. Leitner, A. Michlmayr, F. Rosenberg, S. Dustdar. "Monitoring, prediction and prevention of sla violations in composite services." In: *Proceedings of International Conference on Web Services (ICWS)*. IEEE. 2010, pp. 369–376 (cit. on p. 50).

[Lou06]   P. Louridas. "Static code analysis." In: *IEEE Software* 23.4 (2006), pp. 58–61 (cit. on p. 106).

[LWR+10] P. Leitner, B. Wetzstein, F. Rosenberg, A. Michlmayr, S. Dustdar, F. Leymann. "Runtime prediction of service level agreement violations for composite services." In: *Service-Oriented Computing. ICSOC/Service-Wave 2009 Workshops*. Springer. 2010, pp. 176–186 (cit. on p. 50).

[LWZG09] X. Lu, H. Wang, R. Zhou, B. Ge. "Using Hessian Locally Linear Embedding for autonomic failure prediction." In: *Proceedings of World Congress on Nature & Biologically Inspired Computing (NaBIC)*. IEEE. 2009, pp. 772–776 (cit. on p. 51).

[LZXS07a] Y. Liang, Y. Zhang, H. Xiong, R. Sahoo. "An adaptive semantic filter for Blue Gene/L failure log analysis." In: *Proceedings of Symposium of International Parallel and Distributed Processing (IPDPS)*. IEEE. 2007, pp. 1–8 (cit. on pp. 86, 88–90).

[LZXS07b]   Y. Liang, Y. Zhang, H. Xiong, R. Sahoo. "Failure prediction in IBM BlueGene/L event logs." In: *Proceedings of the 7th International Conference on Data Mining (ICDM)*. IEEE. 2007, pp. 583–588 (cit. on pp. 54, 226).

[MA01]   D. A. Menasce, V. Almeida. *Capacity Planning for Web Services: Metrics, Models, and Methods*. 1st. Prentice Hall, 2001 (cit. on p. 38).

[Mer14]   D. Merkel. "Docker: lightweight linux containers for consistent development and deployment." In: *Linux Journal* 2014.239 (2014), p. 2 (cit. on p. 141).

[MHK05]   J. F. Murray, G. F. Hughes, K. Kreutz-Delgado. "Machine learning methods for predicting failures in hard drives: A multiple-instance application." In: *Journal of Machine Learning research* 6 (2005), p. 816 (cit. on p. 192).

[Moh12]   A. Mohamed. "Software Architecture-Based Failure Prediction." In: (2012) (cit. on p. 58).

[MRH09]   D. C. Montgomery, G. C. Runger, N. F. Hubele. *Engineering statistics*. John Wiley & Sons, 2009 (cit. on pp. 85, 153, 154).

[MS10]   J. P. Magalhaes, L. M. Silva. "Prediction of performance anomalies in web-applications based-on software aging scenarios." In: *Proceedings of the 2nd International Workshop on Software Aging and Rejuvenation (WoSAR)*. IEEE. 2010, pp. 1–7 (cit. on p. 51).

[MT00]   N. Medvidović, R. N. Taylor. "A Classification and Comparison Framework for Software Architecture Description Languages." In: *IEEE Transaction on Software Engineering* 26.1 (Jan. 2000), pp. 70–93 (cit. on p. 37).

[Mus98]   J. D. Musa. *Software reliability engineering*. McGraw-Hill, 1998 (cit. on p. 47).

[NAC11]   N. Nakka, A. Agrawal, A. Choudhary. "Predicting node failure in high performance computing systems from failure and usage logs." In: *Proceedings of International Symposium on Parallel and Distributed Processing Workshops and Phd Forum (IPDPSW)*. IEEE. 2011, pp. 1557–1566 (cit. on p. 56).

[NCM16]   R. Natella, D. Cotroneo, H. S. Madeira. "Assessing Dependability with Software Fault Injection: A Survey." In: *ACM Computing Surveys (CSUR)* 48.3 (2016), p. 44 (cit. on p. 177).

[New15]   S. Newman. *Building Microservices*. 1st. O'Reilly Media, 2015 (cit. on pp. 37, 156, 178).

[Nyg18]   M. Nygard. *Release It!: Design and Deploy Production-Ready Software*. Pragmatic Bookshelf, 2018 (cit. on pp. 2, 5, 236).

[Obj05]   Object Management Group (OMG). *UML Profile for Schedulability, Performance, & Time*. OMG Document Number formal/05-01-02 (`http://www.omg.org/spec/SPTP/`). Jan. 2005 (cit. on p. 39).

[Obj11]   Object Management Group (OMG). *UML Profile for MARTE: Modeling and Analysis of Real-Time Embedded Systems*. OMG Document Number formal/11-06-02 (`http://www.omg.org/spec/MARTE/`). June 2011 (cit. on p. 39).

[OP95]   E. Ottem, J. Plummer. *Playing it SMART: The emergence of reliability prediction technology*. Tech. rep. Technical report, Seagate Technology Paper, 1995 (cit. on pp. 50, 95).

[OS07]   A. Oliner, J. Stearley. "What Supercomputers Say: A Study of Five System Logs." In: *Proceedings of the 37th Annual IEEE/IFIP International Conference on Dependable Systems and Networks (DSN)*. IEEE, 2007, pp. 575–584 (cit. on pp. 86, 89, 91, 180).

[PGK+14]   T. Pitakrat, J. Grunert, O. Kabierschke, F. Keller, A. van Hoorn. "A framework for system event classification and prediction by means of machine learning." In: *Proceedings of the 8th International Conference on Performance Evaluation Methodologies and Tools (VALUETOOLS)*. ICST (Institute for Computer Sciences, Social-Informatics and Telecommunications Engineering). 2014, pp. 173–180 (cit. on pp. X, 2, 72).

[PHG13]   T. Pitakrat, A. van Hoorn, L. Grunske. "A comparison of machine learning algorithms for proactive hard disk drive failure detection." In: *Proceedings of the 4th International ACM Sigsoft Symposium on Architecting Critical Systems (ISARCS)*. ACM. 2013, pp. 1–10 (cit. on pp. X, 72).

[PHG14]   T. Pitakrat, A. van Hoorn, L. Grunske. "Increasing dependability of component-based software systems by online failure prediction (short paper)." In: *Proceedings of the 10th European Dependable Computing Conference (EDCC)*. IEEE. 2014, pp. 66–69 (cit. on pp. IX, 72).

[Pit13]   T. Pitakrat. "Hora: online failure prediction framework for component-based software systems based on Kieker and Palladio." In: *Symposium on Software Performance. Joint Kieker/Palladio Days*. 2013, pp. 39–48 (cit. on p. X).

[Pit18]   T. Pitakrat. *An Architecture-aware Approach to Hierarchical Online Failure Prediction*. May 2018. URL: https://doi.org/10.5281/zenodo.1247872 (cit. on pp. 8, 135, 208, 209, 223).

[Pla99]   J. C. Platt. "Advances in kernel methods." In: Cambridge, MA, USA: MIT Press, 1999. Chap. Fast training of support vector machines using sequential minimal optimization, pp. 185–208 (cit. on p. 26).

[PN05a]   S. Pertet, P. Narasimhan. "Causes of failure in web applications (cmu-pdl-05-109)." In: *Parallel Data Laboratory* (2005), p. 48 (cit. on pp. 161, 178).

[PN05b]   S. Pertet, P. Narasimhan. "Handling cascading failures: the case for topology-aware fault-tolerance." In: *Proceedings of the 1st Workshop on Hot Topics in System Dependability (HotDep)*. Citeseer. 2005 (cit. on p. 59).

[POHG16] T. Pitakrat, D. Okanovic, A. van Hoorn, L. Grunske. "An architecture-aware approach to hierarchical online failure prediction." In: *Proceedings of the 12th International ACM SIGSOFT Conference on Quality of Software Architectures (QoSA)*. IEEE. 2016, pp. 60–69 (cit. on pp. IX, 72).

[POHG18] T. Pitakrat, D. Okanović, A. van Hoorn, L. Grunske. "Hora: Architecture-aware online failure prediction." In: *Journal of Systems and Software* 137 (2018), pp. 669–685 (cit. on pp. IX, 72).

[Qui93]   J. R. Quinlan. *C4.5: Programs for machine learning*. Vol. 1. Morgan Kaufmann, 1993 (cit. on p. 25).

[R C15]   R Core Team. *R: A Language and Environment for Statistical Computing.*
             R Foundation for Statistical Computing. Vienna, Austria, 2015. URL:
             http://www.R-project.org/ (cit. on pp. 139, 143, 154).

[RTH+11]   X. Robin, N. Turck, A. Hainard, N. Tiberti, F. Lisacek, J.-C. Sanchez,
             M. Müller. "pROC: An open-source package for R and S+ to analyze
             and compare ROC curves." In: *BMC bioinformatics* 12.1 (2011), p. 77
             (cit. on p. 154).

[SAG+06]   B. Schmerl, J. Aldrich, D. Garlan, R. Kazman, H. Yan. "Discovering Ar-
             chitectures from Running Systems." In: *IEEE Transactions on Software
             Engineering* 32.7 (July 2006), pp. 454–466 (cit. on p. 101).

[Sch08]   G. Schulmeyer. *Handbook of Software Quality Assurance.* Artech House,
             2008 (cit. on p. 1).

[Scu10]   M. Scutari. "Learning Bayesian Networks with the bnlearn R Package."
             In: *Journal of Statistical Software* 35.3 (2010), pp. 1–22 (cit. on p. 144).

[SFH05]   M. Sumner, E. Frank, M. Hall. "Speeding up Logistic Model Tree
             Induction." In: *Proceedings of the 9th European Conference on Principles
             and Practice of Knowledge Discovery in Databases (PKDD).* Springer,
             2005, pp. 675–683 (cit. on p. 27).

[SLM10]   F. Salfner, M. Lenk, M. Malek. "A survey of online failure prediction
             methods." In: *ACM Computing Surveys* 42.3 (Mar. 2010), 10:1–10:42
             (cit. on pp. 2, 12, 14, 15, 17, 18, 22, 47, 48, 150, 152).

[SM07]   F. Salfner, M. Malek. "Using hidden semi-markov models for effective
             online failure prediction." In: *Proceedings of the 26th International Sym-
             posium on Reliable Distributed Systems (SRDS).* IEEE. 2007, pp. 161–
             174 (cit. on pp. 2, 226).

[SRSD04]   M. Sahinoglu, C. Ramamoorthy, A. E. Smith, B. Dengiz. "A reliability
             block diagramming tool to describe networks." In: *Annual Reliability
             and Maintainability Symposium (RAMS).* IEEE. 2004, pp. 141–145
             (cit. on p. 39).

[SS11]   R. H. Shumway, D. S. Stoffer. *Time Series Analysis and Its Applications:
             With R Examples.* 3rd. Springer Texts in Statistics. Springer, 2011 (cit.
             on pp. 18, 19, 21, 22, 84).

[Sve11]   P. A. Svendsen. "Online failure prediction in UNIX systems." MA thesis. University of Agder, 2011 (cit. on p. 51).

[SWC03]   J. A. Stafford, A. L. Wolf, M. Caporuscio. "The Application of Dependence Analysis to Software Architecture Descriptions." In: *Formal Methods for Software Architectures: Third International School on Formal Methods for the Design of Computer, Communication and Software Systems: Software Architectures (SFM)*. Springer, 2003, pp. 52–62 (cit. on p. 36).

[SWM12]   M. Sonoda, Y. Watanabe, Y. Matsumoto. "Prediction of failure occurrence time based on system log message pattern learning." In: *Proceedings of Network Operations and Management Symposium (NOMS)*. IEEE. 2012, pp. 578–581 (cit. on p. 56).

[SZ13]   A. Shalan, M. Zulkernine. "Runtime Prediction of Failure Modes from System Error Logs." In: *Proceedings of the 18th International Conference on Engineering of Complex Computer Systems (ICECCS)*. IEEE. 2013, pp. 232–241 (cit. on p. 56).

[Szy02]   C. Szyperski. *Component Software: Beyond Object-Oriented Programming*. 2nd. Addison-Wesley Longman, 2002 (cit. on p. 34).

[Tia05]   J. Tian. *Software quality engineering: testing, quality assurance, and quantifiable improvement*. John Wiley & Sons, 2005 (cit. on p. 1).

[TMD09]   R. N. Taylor, N. Medvidović, E. M. Dashofy. *Software Architecture: Foundations, Theory, and Practice*. Wiley Publishing, 2009 (cit. on pp. 5, 33–37).

[TZB11]   N. Theera-Ampornpunt, B. Zhou, S. Bagchi. "Predicting Time to Failure for Large Scale Distributed Systems." In: *Proceedings of the 42nd Annual IEEE/IFIP International Conference On Dependable Systems And Networks (DSN)*. 2011, pp. 27–30 (cit. on p. 55).

[UT14]   J. Uhle, P. Tröger. "On Dependability Modeling in a Deployed Microservice Architecture." MA thesis. Universität Potsdam, 2014 (cit. on p. 57).

[VD02]   R. Vilalta, Y. Drissi. "A Perspective View and Survey of Meta-Learning." In: *Artificial Intelligence Review* 18 (2 2002), pp. 77–95 (cit. on p. 25).

[Wal06]   R. Walker. "Examining Load Average." In: *Linux Journal* 2006.152 (2006), pp. 5–16 (cit. on pp. 83, 163).

[WFHP16]   I. H. Witten, E. Frank, M. A. Hall, C. J. Pal. *Data Mining: Practical machine learning tools and techniques*. Morgan Kaufmann, 2016 (cit. on pp. 139, 181, 189, 194).

[WMCT14]   Y. Wang, E. Ma, T. Chow, K.-L. Tsui. "A Two-Step Parametric Method for Failure Prediction in Hard Disk Drives." In: *IEEE Transactions on Industrial Informatics* 10.1 (Feb. 2014), pp. 419–430 (cit. on p. 52).

[WOS+12]   Y. Watanabe, H. Otsuka, M. Sonoda, S. Kikuchi, Y. Matsumoto. "Online failure prediction in cloud datacenters by real-time message pattern learning." In: *Proceedings of the 4th International Conference on Cloud Computing Technology and Science (CloudCom)*. IEEE. 2012, pp. 504–511 (cit. on p. 55).

[WPN07]   A. W. Williams, S. M. Pertet, P. Narasimhan. "Tiresias: Black-box failure prediction in distributed systems." In: *Proceedings of International Parallel and Distributed Processing Symposium (IPDPS)*. IEEE. 2007, pp. 1–8 (cit. on p. 2).

[WRH+12]   C. Wohlin, P. Runeson, M. Höst, M. C. Ohlsson, B. Regnell, A. Wesslén. *Experimentation in software engineering*. Springer Science & Business Media, 2012 (cit. on p. 154).

[XSJC09]   K.-X. Xue, L. Su, Y.-F. Jia, K.-Y. Cai. "A neural network approach to forecasting computing-resource exhaustion with workload." In: *Proceedings of the 9th International Conference on Quality Software (QSIC)*. IEEE. 2009, pp. 315–324 (cit. on p. 49).

[YZLC11]   L. Yu, Z. Zheng, Z. Lan, S. Coghlan. "Practical online failure prediction for Blue Gene/P: Period-based vs event-driven." In: *Proceedings of the 41st International Conference on Dependable Systems and Networks Workshops (DSN-W)*. IEEE. 2011, pp. 259–264 (cit. on p. 54).

[ZLG+10]   Z. Zheng, Z. Lan, R. Gupta, S. Coghlan, P. Beckman. "A practical failure prediction with location and lead time for Blue Gene/P." In: *Proceedings of International Conference on Dependable Systems and Networks Workshops (DSN-W)*. IEEE. 2010, pp. 15–22 (cit. on p. 54).

[ZWL+13]   B. Zhu, G. Wang, X. Liu, D. Hu, S. Lin, J. Ma. "Proactive drive failure prediction for large scale storage systems." In: *Proceedings of the 29th Symposium on Mass Storage Systems and Technologies (MSST)*. May 2013, pp. 1–5 (cit. on p. 50).

All URLs were last checked on 10.06.2018.

LIST OF FIGURES

LIST OF TABLES